THE BIG BOOK OF EASY SUPPERS

THE
BIG
BOO

270 Delicious Recipes

for Casual Everyday Cooking

OF EASY SUPPERS

K

BY MARYANA VOLLSTEDT

CHRONICLE BOOKS

SAN FRANCISCO

Library of Congress Cataloging-in-Publication
Data available.

ISBN 0-8118-4350-5

Manufactured in Canada.

Designed by George McCalman
Prop styling by Leigh Noe
Food styling by Dan Becker
Photo Assistant by Guarina Lopez
Typesetting by Janis Reed

Distributed in Canada by Raincoast Books
9050 Shaughnessy Street
Vancouver, British Colombia V6P 6E5

10 9 8 7 6 5 4 3 2 1

Chronicle Books LLC
85 Second Street
San Francisco, California 94105

www.chroniclebooks.com

DEDICATION

As always, I dedicate this book to my husband, Reed, who is my adviser, tester, shopper, computer person, confidant, manager, and best friend. He has encouraged and supported me throughout my many years of writing cookbooks. It has really been a team effort, and I couldn't have written them without him. Thank you, Reed. Also to Julie, Scott, Gregg, and Jon, who, for as long as they can remember, have been eating their mother's test recipes.

ACKNOWLEDGMENTS

Thanks again to Bill LeBlond, editorial director of cookbooks at Chronicle Books, for his continued support for my *Big Book* series. *The Big Book of Easy Suppers* follows *The Big Book of Potluck*, *The Big Book of Breakfast*, *The Big Book of Soups & Stews*, and my all-time best-seller, *The Big Book of Casseroles*. To Amy Treadwell at Chronicle Books for her continued help and advice during the writing of the book; to Carrie Bradley for her expert copyediting, additions, and suggestions; and to all of the Chronicle Books staff.

Special thanks to Brian Crow for his computer consulting. I am also grateful to neighbors, friends, and family who were willing testers.

CONTENTS

INTRODUCTION

The Big Book of Easy Suppers offers an alternative to full-course, time-consuming meals with casual, lighter, and fun suppers for family and friends. Featured are main-course soups; salads and sandwiches; easy meat, poultry, and seafood entrées; hearty pastas; egg dishes; healthful stir-fries; grilling recipes; and simple desserts.

Included are a variety of recipes that are generally easy to make, with straightforward directions and ingredients that are, for the most part, already in your pantry or readily available in local supermarkets. Fresh seasonal ingredients are used if available and practical, along with a few convenience foods and some top quality canned foods. Prepared mixes and canned soups are not included in the belief that homemade is truly best.

In some parts of the country, the evening meal is still traditionally called "supper," while "dinner," the biggest meal, is eaten at midday. Many of our grandparents and older folks referred to supper as the casual meal served at the end of a typical day; dinner was a more formal affair reserved for special occasions or after church. My childhood memories of suppers include light meals on Sunday evenings consisting of sandwiches made from leftover roast and served on a teacart in front of the fireplace (no television in those days!).

With today's emphasis on simpler, lighter meals and easy-to-prepare quality food, *The Big Book of Easy Suppers* will appeal to the home cook.

Suppers are ideal to serve for family meals and for informal entertaining. A well-designed supper can be made up of an entrée with perhaps one complementary side dish, and should be wholesome and satisfying.

To save time in preparing quick, easy suppers, it is important to have a well-stocked pantry. Items to always have on hand are flour, sugars, coarse salt, pastas, grains like rice and barley, an assortment of dried legumes and beans, potatoes, onions, and garlic, along with a well-maintained spice rack. Extras, such as canned or dried chiles, hot sauces, flavored vinegars and oils, nuts, olives, anchovies, and sun-dried tomatoes, are fun to have on hand and an easy way to add interest to dishes.

Essential kitchen tools are also necessary in preparing easy suppers. Besides the basic measuring cups and spoons, whisks, spatulas, a good can opener, and several sharp knives, other helpful equipment includes a food processor or blender, heavy skillets in two or three sizes, a sauté pan, two saucepans, a Dutch oven, a heavy-duty baking sheet or two, a kitchen scale, assorted glass baking dishes, a pepper mill for fresh grinding, cake and pie pans for dessert, and plenty of kitchen towels for cleanup.

Enjoy *The Big Book of Easy Suppers*, I hope it will make your life easier, tastier, and more fun at supper time.

CHAPTER 1

MEALS IN A BOWL

Supper soups are satisfying and filling for a complete meal. They often take only one pot to make and one bowl to serve. They are easy to make, generally inexpensive, and healthful. There is nothing more appealing than a savory, bubbling soup simmering on the stove on a cold winter night.

Very little special equipment is needed for soup making: a large soup pot with a lid, a soup ladle, soup spoons, and soup bowls.

In this chapter, you will find a variety of soups that include meats, poultry, seafood, vegetables, pasta, and legumes. Most soups make a large quantity and can be served for two meals—they're often even better the next day. Cooking times are given, but most soups will patiently withstand longer simmering until ready to serve.

For a hot, homemade, no-fuss supper, try a pot of spicy Chili Soup (page 15), Vegetable-Beef Soup with Barley (page 12), Salmon Chowder (page 24), Sausage and Cannellini Bean Soup (page 22), or Hamburger Noodle Soup (page 14), among other warming combinations.

VEGETABLE-BEEF SOUP WITH BARLEY

Serves 8

Don't let the long ingredient list for this soup discourage you—it goes together fast. Full of tender meat, a hearty grain, and winter vegetables, this savory soup will fortify the soul. Allow about 1 ½ hours for simmering to develop the flavors. Serve with some crusty bread.

In a large Dutch oven over medium-high heat, warm oil. Add steak, onion, and garlic and sauté until meat is browned, about 10 minutes. Add celery, carrots, turnip, and bell pepper and mix well. Add broth, tomato juice, tomatoes, Worcestershire sauce, water, barley, and seasonings. Bring soup to a boil over high heat. Reduce heat to medium-low and simmer, covered, 1 hour and 15 minutes. Add peas and simmer, uncovered, until peas are cooked, about 10 minutes longer. Discard bay leaf and serve in bowls.

1 tablespoon vegetable oil

1¼ pounds round steak, cut into ½-inch pieces (see Note, page 249) or stew meat

1 cup chopped yellow onion

2 garlic cloves, minced

2 celery stalks, sliced

2 carrots, sliced

1 small turnip, peeled and cubed

1 green or red bell pepper, seeded and cut into bite-sized pieces

3 cups beef broth

3 cups tomato juice

1 can (14½ ounces) whole tomatoes, with juice, cut up

1 teaspoon Worcestershire sauce

1 cup water

½ cup barley, rinsed

1 teaspoon chili powder

½ teaspoon dried thyme

1 bay leaf

1¼ teaspoons salt

Freshly ground pepper to taste

1 cup peas, fresh or frozen

ALPHABET SOUP

Serves 6

Have fun with your family and serve this healthful soup for supper. Vegetables add color, as well as essential vitamins and minerals. Kids like to find their names in the soup.

In a large Dutch oven over medium heat, combine beef, onion, and garlic and sauté, breaking up meat with a spoon, until meat is browned and onion and garlic are tender, about 5 minutes, adding a little oil if needed. Add tomatoes, tomato sauce, tomato juice, broth, water, seasonings, carrots, celery, and zucchini. Bring to a boil over high heat. Reduce heat to medium-low and simmer, covered, 20 minutes. Add peas and pasta and cook until pasta is tender, about 10 minutes longer. Serve in bowls.

½   pound ground beef or ground turkey
½   cup chopped yellow onion
1   garlic clove, minced
    Vegetable oil, as needed
1   can (15 ounces) diced tomatoes, with juice
1   can (8 ounces) tomato sauce
1½ cups tomato juice
1   can (10½ ounces) beef broth, undiluted
2   cups water
¼   teaspoon dried basil
¼   teaspoon dried oregano
¾   teaspoon salt
    Freshly ground pepper to taste
2   carrots, chopped
1   celery stalk, chopped
½   zucchini, unpeeled, chopped
¾   cup peas, fresh or frozen
⅓   cup alphabet pasta

HAMBURGER NOODLE SOUP

Serves 4

A new version of an old family favorite and a great warmer-upper on chilly days. Open faced cheese sandwiches are a good accompaniment to serve with this soup.

In a large soup pot or Dutch oven over medium heat, combine beef, onion, bell pepper, and garlic and sauté, breaking up meat with a spoon, until meat is browned and vegetables are tender, about 5 minutes, adding a little oil if needed. Add remaining ingredients except noodles and simmer, uncovered, about 10 minutes. Discard bay leaf. Increase heat to medium-high and add noodles. Cook until noodles are tender and flavors are blended, about 10 minutes longer. Serve in bowls.

1   pound ground beef or ground turkey
1   cup chopped yellow onion
½   cup chopped green bell pepper
1   garlic clove, minced
    Vegetable oil, as needed
1   can (14½ ounces) whole tomatoes, with juices, cut up
2   cans (14½ ounces each) beef broth
1   can (8 ounces) tomato sauce
2   cups tomato juice
½   teaspoon dried basil
1   bay leaf
1¼ teaspoons salt
    Freshly ground pepper to taste
¼   cup chopped fresh parsley
1½ cups egg noodles, slightly broken

CHILI SOUP

Serves 8

Serve this chili-type soup for a game-watching supper with cold beer, crudités, and chips. The toppings make it fun and add flavor. Your family or guests won't pass up Easy Brownies (page 326) for dessert.

In a large soup pot over medium heat, combine beef and onion and sauté, breaking up meat with a spoon, until meat is browned and onion is tender, about 5 minutes, adding a little oil if needed. Add remaining ingredients except toppings. Reduce heat to medium-low and simmer, uncovered, until flavors are blended, 20 to 30 minutes. Serve in bowls and pass the toppings.

½   pound ground beef

1   cup chopped yellow onion
    Vegetable oil, as needed

3   cans (14½ ounces each) beef broth

1   can (14½ ounces) whole tomatoes, with juice, cut up

1   can (15 ounces) kidney beans, drained and rinsed

1½ teaspoons chili powder

¾   teaspoon salt

¼   teaspoon freshly ground pepper

TOPPINGS

Sour cream

Grated Cheddar cheese

Chopped green onions

THREE-BEAN CHILI WITH MEAT
Serves 8

This spicy chili with a variety of beans and a choice of toppings will brighten up a rainy day. Corn bread makes a good accompaniment. Invite the neighbors for supper—this recipe makes a lot. For vegetarians, omit the meat and add 1 to 2 cups fresh or frozen corn kernels.

In a large soup pot over medium heat, combine beef and onion and sauté, breaking up meat with a spoon, until meat is browned and onion is tender, about 5 minutes, adding a little oil if needed. Add remaining ingredients except toppings. Reduce heat to medium-low and simmer, uncovered, until flavors are blended, 20 to 30 minutes. Serve in bowls and pass the toppings.

1   pound ground beef
1   cup chopped yellow onion
1   garlic clove, minced
     Vegetable oil, as needed
1   can (28 ounces) whole tomatoes, with juices, cut up
1   can (15 ounces) tomato sauce
1   can (14½ ounces) beef broth
1   can (15 ounces) black beans, drained and rinsed
2   cans (15 ounces each) red kidney beans, drained and rinsed
1   can (15 ounces) pinto beans, drained and rinsed
1   tablespoon chili powder, or more to taste
¼   teaspoon ground cumin
¾   teaspoon salt
     Freshly ground pepper to taste

TOPPINGS
Grated Monterey Jack or Cheddar cheese
Chopped red or green onions
Sour cream

ZESTY MEATBALLS AND PASTA SOUP

Serves 4 to 6

Zesty chile-cheese meatballs floating in a flavorful broth with pasta make this meal in a bowl filling and give it character. The meatballs take a little time to make, but they are so good, they are worth it. Any kind of pasta strands can be used.

In a large soup pot over high heat, combine broth, tomatoes, onion, garlic, oregano, ½ teaspoon salt, and pepper and bring to a boil. Reduce heat to medium-low and simmer, covered, 10 minutes.

In a medium bowl, combine beef, remaining ¼ teaspoon salt, ¼ cup Parmesan, and chiles. Form into ¾- to 1-inch meatballs (about 16) and add to broth. Add zucchini and pasta and simmer, covered, until meatballs are cooked and zucchini and pasta mixture is tender, about 15 minutes longer. Serve in bowls, sprinkled with Parmesan.

2   cans (14½ ounces each) beef broth

1   can (14½ ounces) whole tomatoes, with juice, cut up

½   cup chopped yellow onion

1   garlic clove, minced

½   teaspoon dried oregano

¾   teaspoon salt
     Freshly ground pepper to taste

¾   pound ground beef

¼   cup freshly grated Parmesan cheese, plus extra for sprinkling

½   can (2 ounces) diced green chiles, drained

½   zucchini, unpeeled, cut into ½-inch dice (about 1 cup)

2   ounces (about ½ cup) angel hair pasta, broken into 1-inch pieces

CREAMY CHICKEN AND MUSHROOM SOUP

Serves 4 to 6

This soup, chock-full of chicken and mushrooms in a broth enriched by sour cream, is outstanding for an evening supper. Serve with warm baguette slices. Homemade chicken broth is best, but high-quality purchased may be used.

In a large soup pot over medium heat, melt butter. Add onion, mushrooms, and bell pepper and sauté until tender, about 5 minutes. Stir in flour. Add broth and stir until slightly thickened, about 2 minutes. Add wine, seasonings, and chicken. Reduce heat to low and simmer, uncovered, 10 minutes. Remove from heat and stir in sour cream until blended. Return pan to heat, but do not boil. Serve in bowls.

¼ cup (½ stick) butter
½ cup chopped yellow onion
8 ounces mushrooms, sliced
½ cup chopped red bell pepper
¼ cup all-purpose flour
3 cups chicken broth
2 tablespoons dry white wine
½ teaspoon dried thyme
½ teaspoon salt
⅛ teaspoon white pepper
1 cup cubed cooked chicken breast (see Note, page 30)
½ cup sour cream

NOTE: If making ahead, reheat slowly over medium-low heat.

MEXICAN CHICKEN SOUP

Serves 6

Black beans and corn add body and substance to this spicy chicken soup that takes the chill off of cold, blustery days. I once made this soup for my neighbor, and he said it was a winner. Serve with warm tortillas.

In a large soup pot over high heat, bring broth, tomatoes, and rice to a boil. Reduce heat to medium-low and cook, covered, until rice is tender, about 20 minutes. Add remaining ingredients except sour cream, lime wedges, and tortillas and cook, uncovered, until heated through and flavors are blended, about 10 minutes. Serve in bowls topped with a dollop of sour cream, and garnish with lime wedges, if desired. Pass the warm tortillas.

4	cups chicken broth
1	can (15 ounces) Mexican stewed tomatoes, with juice, cut up
¼	cup long-grain white rice
1	can (15 ounces) black beans, drained and rinsed
1	cup corn kernels, fresh or frozen
1	cup cubed cooked chicken breast (see Note, page 30)
2	tablespoons tomato salsa
1	tablespoon minced fresh cilantro or parsley
¼	teaspoon ground cumin
¼	teaspoon salt
	Freshly ground pepper to taste
	Sour cream for topping (optional)
	Lime wedges for garnish (optional)
	Warmed flour tortillas (see Note, page 70)

SPLIT PEA SOUP WITH HAM BONE

Serves 6

This is an easy soup to make because split peas do not require presoaking. Just put all of the ingredients in a pot and slowly cook until tender. The ham bone adds a salty flavor and substance to the soup, but the soup can be made without it (see Note).

In a large soup pot over high heat, combine all ingredients and bring to a boil. Reduce heat to medium-low and simmer, uncovered, until peas are soft, about 1 hour. Remove ham bone to a plate and cut off the ham. Discard bay leaf. For a thicker soup, whisk soup with a large whisk to mash some of the peas. Return ham pieces to the soup. Serve in bowls.

1   package (1 pound) split peas (2 cups), rinsed and sorted
8   cups water or a combination of water and chicken broth
1   cup chopped yellow onion
1   or 2 carrots, chopped
1   celery stalk, chopped
1   bay leaf
1/4   teaspoon dried marjoram
1   teaspoon salt
    Freshly ground pepper to taste
1   meaty ham bone, fat removed (optional; see Note)

NOTE: Add more salt to taste if the ham bone is omitted.

LENTIL AND SPLIT PEA SOUP WITH SMOKED SAUSAGE

Serves 4

In about an hour, you will have this healthful, hearty soup on the table for an easy supper. Serve with warm French bread. The soup will get thicker the next day. Omit the sausage for a vegetarian soup.

In a large soup pot over high heat, combine all ingredients except sausage, salt, pepper, and vinegar and bring to a boil. Reduce heat to medium-low and simmer, uncovered, 30 minutes, stirring occasionally. Add sausage and cook, uncovered, until peas and lentils are tender, 30 minutes longer. Season with salt and pepper and stir in vinegar. Discard bay leaf. For a thicker soup, whisk soup with a large whisk to mash some of the peas and lentils. Serve in bowls.

1 cup brown lentils, rinsed and sorted
1 cup split peas, rinsed and sorted
8 cups water
1 cup chopped yellow onion
1 celery stalk, sliced
2 garlic cloves, minced
2 carrots, sliced
1 bay leaf
½ teaspoon dried thyme
½ teaspoon dried oregano
¼ teaspoon ground cumin
8 ounces smoked sausage, sliced
Salt and freshly ground pepper to taste
1 tablespoon red wine vinegar

SAUSAGE AND CANNELLINI BEAN SOUP

Serves 4

This satisfying one-dish offering combines sausage and beans in a flavorful broth. Serve with garlic bread.

In a large soup pot over medium heat, combine sausage, leeks, and garlic and sauté, breaking up meat with a spoon, until meat is browned and vegetables are tender, 6 to 7 minutes, adding a little oil if needed. Add beans, broth, tomatoes, parsley, basil, salt, and pepper. Reduce heat to medium-low and simmer, uncovered, 10 to 15 minutes. Serve in bowls, sprinkled with Parmesan.

½ pound bulk Italian sausage

2 large leeks, white parts only, well rinsed and coarsely chopped

2 garlic cloves, minced

Vegetable oil, as needed

1 can (15 ounces) cannellini beans or other white beans, drained and rinsed

3 cups chicken broth

1 can (14½ ounces) crushed tomatoes in rich purée

2 tablespoons chopped fresh parsley

½ teaspoon dried basil

½ teaspoon salt

Freshly ground pepper to taste

Freshly grated Parmesan cheese for sprinkling

WINTER VEGETABLE SOUP WITH KIELBASA, PASTA, AND BEANS

Serves 6 to 8

Cozy up to the fireplace with this thick, chunky soup that is almost like a stew. This soup delivers fresh flavors and a balance of textures with meat, vegetables, beans, and pasta. Serve with crusty bread.

In a large soup pot over medium heat, warm oil. Add kielbasa and onion and sauté until onion is tender, about 5 minutes. Raise temperature to high. Add broth, carrots, squash, salt, and pepper and bring to a boil. Reduce heat to medium-low and simmer, uncovered, until vegetables are tender, about 15 minutes. Add beans and macaroni and simmer until macaroni is tender, about 15 minutes longer. Add spinach and cook until spinach is wilted, about 5 minutes longer, stirring several times. Serve in bowls.

1   tablespoon vegetable oil

½   pound kielbasa, cut into ¼-inch slices and halved

1   cup chopped yellow onion

3   cans (14½ ounces each) chicken broth

2   carrots, sliced

1   pound butternut squash, peeled and cubed

½   teaspoon salt

     Freshly ground pepper to taste

1   can (15 ounces) red kidney beans, drained and rinsed

4   ounces (about ¾ cup) small macaroni

4   ounces fresh spinach, chopped, or ½ package (5 ounces) frozen spinach, thawed and squeezed dry

SALMON CHOWDER

Serves 4

This chunky chowder features salmon along with the classic potatoes, onions, and creamy broth, but other seafood can be used. This is a convenient soup to make because most of the ingredients are good pantry items.

In a large soup pot over medium heat, combine onion, celery, potatoes, and water. Bring to a simmer and cook, covered, until vegetables are tender, about 10 minutes. Stir in flour and blend. Add milk, dill, salt, pepper, and salmon and mix well. Bring to a boil, stirring constantly, then reduce heat to medium-low and simmer, uncovered, until flavors are blended, about 15 minutes longer. If desired, mash some of the potatoes with the back of a spoon for a thicker soup. Serve in bowls with a pat of butter, paprika, and parsley on top.

1   cup chopped yellow onion

1   celery stalk, cut into ½-inch slices

3   large russet potatoes (about 1½ pounds), peeled and sliced (about 4 cups)

1   cup water

2   tablespoons all-purpose flour

2½ cups whole milk

¼   teaspoon dried dill

¾   teaspoon salt

Freshly ground pepper to taste

2   cans (6 ounces each) skinless and boneless salmon, drained and flaked, or 1½ cups flaked cooked fresh salmon

2   tablespoons butter

Paprika for sprinkling on top

Chopped fresh parsley for sprinkling on top

VARIATIONS
Clam Chowder: Omit salmon and add 1 to 2 cans (7 ounces each) chopped clams with juice.
Seafood Chowder: Omit salmon and add 1 cup cooked, flaked fish and ½ cup small cooked shrimp.

VEGETARIAN MINESTRONE
Serves 8

Thick with beans and vegetables, this hearty soup is nourishing and tasty but low in calories and fat. Serve in large bowls and sprinkle generously with freshly grated Parmesan cheese. It's even better the next day!

In a large soup pot over high heat, combine tomatoes, tomato juice, broth, 2 cups water, onion, carrots, celery, cabbage, basil, thyme, oregano, salt, and pepper. Bring to a boil, reduce heat to medium-low, and simmer, covered, 30 minutes. Add beans, parsley, zucchini, and macaroni and simmer, covered, until macaroni and vegetables are tender, about 15 minutes longer. Serve in bowls, sprinkled with Parmesan.

1   can (14½ ounces) whole tomatoes, with juice, cut up
3   cups tomato juice
2   cups vegetable broth or water
2   cups water
1   small yellow onion, chopped
2   carrots, sliced
2   celery stalks, sliced
2   cups chopped green cabbage
1   teaspoon dried basil
½   teaspoon dried thyme
½   teaspoon dried oregano
1   teaspoon salt
    Freshly ground pepper to taste
2   cans (15 ounces each) cannellini beans, drained and rinsed
¼   cup chopped fresh parsley
1   medium zucchini, unpeeled, quartered lengthwise, and sliced
¾   cup macaroni or other small pasta
    Freshly grated Parmesan cheese for sprinkling

MAIN-COURSE SUPPER

SALADS

CHAPTER 2

SENSATIONAL STAND-ALONE SALADS

Main-course salads are the perfect supper to serve when time is short or it's too hot to cook. The recipes in this chapter combine meats, seafood, or poultry with greens or other complementary ingredients. Supper salads are hearty and filling and easy to make. Using homemade dressings will improve the flavor and quality of the salad. They are superior to most purchased dressings, and are also economical.

No special equipment is needed, just a large bowl and servers. A salad spinner is nice to have for speedy drying of greens.

With menus from Chicken and Pasta Salad with Blueberries (page 33), Seafood Salad (page 38), Tarragon Chicken Salad (page 30), Grilled Flank Steak and Mixed Greens (page 29), and Classic Chef's Salad (page 36) to Shrimp and Pasta Salad (page 39) there is a fresh, filling supper here for every preference.

CONTINENTAL SALAD

Serves 6

This hearty salad is a perfect use for leftover beef, combined with fresh vegetables and mixed with a tangy horseradish dressing.

In a medium saucepan over medium-high heat, bring just enough lightly salted water to cover potatoes to a boil. Add potatoes, reduce heat to medium and cook, covered, until tender, 15 to 20 minutes. Cool and slice, but do not peel.

In a medium bowl, toss together potatoes, onion, celery, bell pepper, and beef with enough dressing to coat. Cover and refrigerate several hours. Arrange beef mixture evenly among 6 lettuce-lined plates. Garnish with egg quarters, tomato wedges, olives, and pickles.

3   medium unpeeled new potatoes (about 1 pound), scrubbed and halved

1/4   cup chopped red onion

3/4   cup chopped celery

1/2   red bell pepper, seeded and cut into bite-sized pieces

2   cups cooked roast beef (about 1 pound), cut into bite-sized pieces

    Horseradish Dressing (recipe follows)

    Red lettuce leaves for lining plates

2   large hard-cooked eggs, peeled and quartered

2   tomatoes, cut into wedges

1/2   cup pitted black olives

6   gherkin pickles

HORSERADISH DRESSING

In a medium bowl, whisk together all ingredients. Cover and refrigerate until ready to use.

Makes about 1 cup

1/2   cup mayonnaise

1/4   cup buttermilk

1   tablespoon prepared horseradish, or more to taste

1   teaspoon ground mustard

1/2   teaspoon salt

1/8   teaspoon freshly ground pepper

GRILLED FLANK STEAK AND MIXED GREENS

Serves 6 to 8

The addition of hearty steak strips turns a tossed green salad into a satisfying supper salad. Serve with warm French bread.

In an 8-by-10-inch glass baking dish, place flank steak and 1/4 cup of the dressing and turn to coat. Cover and refrigerate several hours, turning once. Bring to room temperature before grilling.

Prepare grill. Grill steak over high heat until medium-rare, 12 to 15 minutes, or to desired doneness, turning once. Transfer steak to a cutting board and let stand 5 minutes. Slice on the diagonal across the grain into 3/8-inch strips.

In a large bowl, toss greens and mushrooms with the remaining dressing to coat. Arrange greens on a large platter or on individual plates. Top with meat strips and garnish with tomato wedges.

1   flank steak (about 1 1/2 pounds)
    Herbed Garlicky Dressing (recipe follows)
8   to 10 cups mixed salad greens
8   ounces mushrooms, sliced
2   tomatoes, cut into wedges

HERBED GARLICKY DRESSING

In a small bowl, whisk together all ingredients. Cover and refrigerate until ready to use.

Makes about 1/2 cup

1/2   cup olive oil
2 1/2 tablespoons red wine vinegar
2   teaspoons Dijon mustard
3   garlic cloves, minced
1/4   teaspoon dried oregano
1/4   teaspoon dried basil
1/4   teaspoon salt
1/8   teaspoon freshly ground pepper

TARRAGON CHICKEN SALAD

Serves 4

A creamy tarragon dressing adds complementary flavors to this elegant salad made with cubes of tender chicken or turkey breast. It is a great way to use leftovers. Serve with warm croissants.

In a medium bowl, combine chicken, onion, celery, mushrooms, and parsley. Toss with enough dressing to coat. Cover and refrigerate several hours to allow flavors to blend.

To serve, divide salad greens equally among individual plates and top with chicken mixture.

2½ cups cubed cooked chicken or turkey breast (see Note)

¼   cup chopped red onion

½   cup chopped celery

3   ounces mushrooms, coarsely chopped

2   tablespoons chopped fresh parsley

4   cups mixed salad greens
    Creamy Tarragon Dressing (page 46)

NOTE: To cook chicken breasts, use either skinned and boned chicken breasts or breasts with bone in and skin on. (The bones and skin add extra flavor.) Put chicken breasts in a saucepan and add enough water or chicken stock to cover. For 2 chicken breast halves, add a pinch of salt, 1 parsley sprig, 1 small chunk of onion, and 2 or 3 black peppercorns. Bring to a boil over high heat, immediately reduce to low, and simmer (liquid should barely bubble), covered, until chicken turns white, about 15 minutes. Transfer chicken to a plate to cool until ready to use, or cool in liquid if time allows. Remove any skin and bones, if necessary, and discard. The broth may be strained and refrigerated or frozen for other uses. One ½-pound chicken breast half will yield 1 cup of diced cooked chicken.

CURRIED CHICKEN, ARTICHOKE, AND RICE SALAD

Serves 4

The light curry dressing binds the ingredients together in this enticing main-course supper salad. Served with Exotic Fruit Salad (page 61), this was one of the favorites at a tasting party.

In a medium bowl, combine all ingredients and toss with enough dressing to coat. Cover and refrigerate several hours to allow the flavors to blend. If the salad seems dry, add a little more dressing or mayonnaise before serving.

½ cup long-grain white rice, cooked according to package directions (1½ cups cooked)

4 green onions, including some tender green tops, sliced

2 cups cubed cooked chicken or roasted turkey breast (see Note, page 30)

¼ cup diced red bell pepper

¼ cup diced celery

1 jar (6½ ounces) marinated quartered artichoke hearts, drained and cut into bite-sized pieces (reserve 2 tablespoons of the marinade for the dressing)

Curry Dressing (recipe follows)

CURRY DRESSING

In a small bowl, whisk together all ingredients until smooth. Cover and refrigerate until ready to use.

Makes about ⅔ cup

¼ cup mayonnaise

¼ cup plain nonfat yogurt

2 tablespoons reserved artichoke marinade

½ to 1 teaspoon curry powder, to taste

¼ teaspoon salt

⅛ teaspoon freshly ground pepper

CHICKEN AND FRESH STRAWBERRY SALAD

Serves 4

Make this salad in the summer, when juicy ripe berries are in season, for a summer supper on the deck. Serve with cheese bread.

In a large bowl, whisk together mayonnaise, vinegar, chutney, curry powder, salt, and pepper. Add remaining ingredients except strawberries and lettuce and toss to mix well. Cover and refrigerate several hours to allow flavors to blend. Just before serving, gently fold in sliced strawberries. Mound salad on a lettuce-lined platter or divide among individual plates. Garnish with whole berries.

1   cup mayonnaise

2   tablespoons white wine vinegar

2   tablespoons chutney, preferably Major Gray's

½   to 1 teaspoon curry powder, to taste

½   teaspoon salt

   Freshly ground pepper to taste

2   cups cubed cooked chicken breast (see Note, page 30)

1   cup chopped celery

6   green onions, including some tender green tops, sliced

¼   cup chopped walnuts

2½ cups hulled and sliced fresh strawberries, plus 8 whole strawberries for garnish

   Lettuce leaves for lining platter

CHICKEN AND PASTA SALAD WITH BLUEBERRIES

Serves 6

For a light summer supper, serve this healthful salad with warm croissants and a plate of cantaloupe spears and watermelon chunks.

In a large bowl, toss pasta with oil. Cover and refrigerate until cool. Add remaining ingredients except blueberries and almonds and toss with enough dressing to coat. Cover and chill several hours to allow flavors to blend. Just before serving, fold in blueberries and sprinkle with almonds.

8   ounces (about 2½ cups) penne, cooked according to package directions and drained

1   tablespoon vegetable oil

2   cups shredded or cubed cooked chicken (see Note, page 30)

½   cup sliced celery

½   cup chopped red bell pepper

3   tablespoons diced red onion

¼   cup chopped fresh parsley

1   cup fresh blueberries, rinsed and dried

¼   cup slivered almonds, toasted (see Note)
    Creamy Tarragon Dressing (page 46)

NOTE: To toast almonds, preheat oven to 350°F. Place nuts on a baking sheet and bake, stirring once, until lightly browned, about 6 minutes. Watch carefully to prevent burning, and transfer immediately to a plate to cool; the nuts will continue to cook while cooling.

PASTA SALAD WITH TURKEY BREAST AND VEGETABLES

Serves 4 to 6

Turkey combined with pasta makes a satisfying and filling salad. You can use leftover turkey or buy good-quality roasted turkey breast at the deli section of the supermarket.

In a large bowl, toss pasta with oil, vinegar, and thyme and mix well. Cover and refrigerate until cool. Add turkey, celery, bell pepper, and green onions and toss with enough dressing to coat. Cover and chill several hours to allow flavors to blend.

8	ounces fusilli (2½ cups), cooked according to package directions and drained
1	tablespoon vegetable oil
2	tablespoons white wine vinegar
½	teaspoon dried thyme
2	cups cubed roasted turkey breast
½	cup chopped celery
½	cup chopped red bell pepper
¼	cup sliced green onions, including some tender green tops
	Creamy Dressing (recipe follows)

CREAMY DRESSING

In a small bowl, whisk together all ingredients until smooth. Cover and refrigerate until ready to use.

Makes about ¾ cup

½	cup mayonnaise
¼	cup sour cream or plain nonfat yogurt
1	tablespoon white wine vinegar
¼	teaspoon dried chervil or basil
¼	teaspoon salt
	Freshly ground pepper to taste

TURKEY SALAD WITH DRIED CRANBERRIES

Serves 4

This delicious combination of turkey, apples, and cranberries tossed with a creamy dressing was served to me at one of our leading Eugene restaurants. It makes a light supper to serve after the holidays. Serve with warm rolls or croissants. If you prefer, use chicken breast.

In a large bowl, combine all ingredients except lettuce and toss with enough dressing to coat. Cover and refrigerate several hours to allow flavors to blend. To serve, line individual plates with lettuce leaves. Divide turkey mixture evenly among the plates.

3 cups roasted turkey breast, cut into bite-sized pieces

2 small green apples such as Granny Smith, unpeeled, cored and cut into bite-sized pieces

2 tablespoons fresh lemon juice

1/4 cup chopped red onion

1/4 cup dried cranberries

1/4 cup chopped walnuts

Butter lettuce for lining plates

Creamy Dressing (facing page)

CLASSIC CHEF'S SALAD

Serves 4

This popular salad has been featured in restaurants for many years as a main-course salad. Lettuce is topped with strips of cooked chicken or turkey breast, ham, and cheese, with the dressing served on the side. The ingredients should be prepared and chilled well ahead of assembling. Choose one of the dressings offered here, or serve both. Include a basket of warm rolls to complete the meal.

In a large bowl, toss together lettuce, green onions, and celery. Divide evenly among individual plates. Arrange chicken, ham, and cheese strips in rows over the top. Garnish with egg wedges, tomato wedges, and olives. Pass the dressing in a bowl.

NOTE: To slice ham and cheese quickly, stack slices together, and cut into ¼-by-2-inch strips.

6   cups shredded iceberg lettuce

6   green onions, including some tender green tops, sliced

1   celery stalk, sliced

½   pound cooked chicken or roasted turkey breast, cut into narrow strips (about 1½ cups)

½   pound cooked ham, cut into narrow strips (about 1½ cups)

3   ounces Swiss cheese, cut into narrow strips (see Note)

2   hard-cooked eggs, peeled and cut into wedges

2   tomatoes, cut into wedges

½   cup black olives

CHOICE OF DRESSINGS
Oil and Vinegar Dressing (recipe follows)
Super Thousand Island Dressing (page 41)

OIL AND VINEGAR DRESSING

In a small bowl, whisk together all ingredients.

Makes about ¾ cup

½   cup olive oil

¼   cup red wine vinegar

1   garlic clove, minced

¼   teaspoon salt
     Freshly ground pepper to taste

TOSSED GREEN SALAD WITH BAY SHRIMP AND ARTICHOKES

Serves 6

This salad can be served any time of the year for a light supper, as all of the ingredients are readily available. Include some warm, crusty bread.

In a large salad bowl, combine all ingredients and toss with enough dressing to coat.

6   to 8 cups torn romaine lettuce leaves

8   ounces cooked small bay shrimp

1   jar (6 ounces) marinated quartered artichoke hearts, drained and cut into bite-sized pieces

1   cup pitted Kalamata or other black olives

1   tablespoon capers, drained

1   small cucumber, peeled, halved lengthwise, seeded, and sliced

1   cup crumbled feta cheese

Lemon-Dijon Vinaigrette (page 47)

SEAFOOD SALAD

Serves 4

This combination of popular seafood is one you will enjoy for a light supper on a hot summer evening. Serve with sourdough rolls.

In a large bowl, combine all ingredients except lettuce leaves and toss with enough dressing to coat. Taste and adjust seasoning with salt, if desired. Divide mixture evenly among individual lettuce-lined plates.

8   ounces cooked whitefish such as halibut, snapper, or cod, flaked (see Note)

4   ounces cooked small bay shrimp

4   ounces lump crabmeat, picked over and flaked

½   cup chopped celery

½   cup chopped green bell pepper

6   green onions, including some tender green tops, sliced

Lettuce leaves for lining plates

⅓   to ½ cup Super Thousand Island Dressing (page 41)

Salt (optional)

NOTE: To cook fish, place in a saucepan with a small amount of salted water and simmer, covered, until fish turns opaque, about 5 minutes. Cool and flake.

SHRIMP AND PASTA SALAD
Serves 6 to 8

Small shrimp highlights this supper salad with vegetables and pasta tossed with a creamy dill dressing. This salad can be made ahead for a picnic or potluck.

In a large bowl, toss pasta with oil. Cover and refrigerate until cool. Add remaining ingredients to the pasta and toss with enough dressing to coat. Cover and chill several hours to allow flavors to blend. If the salad seems dry, add a little more dressing or mayonnaise before serving.

- 8 ounces (2½ cups) shell pasta, cooked according to package directions and drained
- 1 tablespoon vegetable oil
- 6 green onions, including some tender green tops, thinly sliced
- 1 cup chopped red bell pepper
- 1 cup chopped celery
- 1 avocado, peeled, pitted, and cut into bite-sized pieces
- 12 ounces cooked small bay shrimp
- Creamy Dill Dressing (recipe follows)

CREAMY DILL DRESSING

In a medium bowl, whisk together all ingredients. Cover and refrigerate until ready to use.

Makes about 1 cup

- ¾ cup mayonnaise
- ¼ cup buttermilk
- 1 tablespoon fresh lemon juice
- 1 garlic clove, minced
- 2 tablespoons finely chopped fresh parsley
- 1 tablespoon snipped fresh dill or 1 teaspoon dried dill
- ¼ teaspoon salt
- Freshly ground pepper to taste

CRAB AND SHRIMP LOUIE SALAD

Serves 4

Crab Louie is an all-time supper favorite for a main-course, hot-weather salad. The addition of bay shrimp and artichoke hearts is an extra bonus. Have all the ingredients thoroughly chilled before assembling. Serve with garlic bread and cold beer or iced tea.

Divide lettuce evenly among individual plates. Add crabmeat and shrimp in small mounds on top of the lettuce. Arrange artichoke hearts, tomato wedges, and egg quarters around the outside. Sprinkle avocado slices with lemon juice and divide evenly among the plates. Garnish with olives. Pass the dressing in a small pitcher.

1   small head iceberg lettuce, shredded or torn (about 4 cups)

½   pound lump crabmeat, picked over and flaked

½   pound cooked small bay shrimp

1.   jar (6½ ounces) marinated quartered artichoke hearts, drained

2   tomatoes, seeded and cut into wedges

4   large hard-cooked eggs, peeled and quartered

2   avocados, peeled, pitted, and sliced

1   tablespoon fresh lemon juice

     Pitted black olives for garnish

CHOICE OF DRESSINGS

Super Thousand Island Dressing (recipe on facing page)

Quick Thousand Island Dressing (recipe on facing page)

SUPER THOUSAND ISLAND DRESSING

This dressing is good with any seafood salad.

In a food processor, combine all ingredients and blend until smooth. Cover and refrigerate until ready to use.

Makes about 1 cup

1	cup mayonnaise
1	tablespoon fresh lemon juice
¼	cup chili sauce or ketchup
1	teaspoon prepared horseradish
1	tablespoon sweet pickle relish or 1 sweet pickle, cut up
2	green onions, including some tender green tops, coarsely chopped
1	fresh parsley sprig, torn up
½	teaspoon ground mustard
1	teaspoon Worcestershire sauce
½	teaspoon salt
2	drops Tabasco sauce

QUICK THOUSAND ISLAND DRESSING

In a medium bowl, whisk together all ingredients. Cover and refrigerate until ready to use.

Makes about 1¼ cups

1	cup mayonnaise
¼	cup chili sauce
1	teaspoon Worcestershire sauce
1	teaspoon sweet pickle relish
¼	teaspoon salt

SHRIMP, SCALLOP, AND SUGAR SNAP PEA SALAD WITH SESAME SEED DRESSING

Serves 4 to 6

This composed salad of plump shrimp, succulent scallops, sweet peas, and crisp cucumbers marinated in a sesame seed dressing is an appealing main-course salad. Serve with assorted breads.

In a medium saucepan over medium-high heat, bring just enough water to cover shrimp to a boil. Add shrimp and cook until they turn pink, about 2 minutes. Drain and transfer to a bowl. Cook scallops in the same way, boiling until they turn opaque, about 2 minutes. Drain and add to bowl with shrimp. Pour half of the dressing over and toss to coat. Cover and refrigerate 1 to 2 hours to allow flavors to blend.

Place peas in a colander and pour boiling water over. Drain and dry. Place in another bowl, add cucumber, and toss lightly with remaining dressing. Cover and refrigerate 1 to 2 hours to allow flavors to blend.

Drain peas mixture and seafood and arrange in mounds on a serving platter lined with lettuce leaves. Garnish with cherry tomatoes.

¾ pound large shrimp (15 to 18), shelled and deveined

¾ pound sea scallops (see Note, page 166)

Sesame Seed Dressing (recipe on facing page)

½ pound sugar snap peas (about 2 cups), trimmed

1 cucumber, peeled, halved lengthwise, seeded, and sliced

Lettuce leaves for lining the platter

1 cup cherry tomatoes

SESAME SEED DRESSING

In a small bowl, whisk together all ingredients.

Makes about ¾ cup

½ cup vegetable oil
¼ cup white wine vinegar
1   tablespoon fresh lemon juice
2   tablespoons soy sauce
½ teaspoon ground mustard
¼ teaspoon salt
1   tablespoon sesame seeds, toasted
    (see Note)

NOTE: To toast sesame seeds, place in a small nonstick skillet over medium-high heat and stir constantly until lightly browned, 1 to 2 minutes. Watch carefully to prevent burning and transfer immediately to a plate to cool; the seeds will continue to cook while cooling.

SALAD

CHAPTER 3

SALADS TO ENHANCE ANY MAIN DISH

Side salads should be complementary to the entrée, adding the right flavor and providing contrast in texture and color. Tossed green salads, with a variety of greens and other ingredients and with appropriate dressings, rate high as versatile side salads. Fruit salads are always refreshing, especially in the summer when fresh fruit is in season. Pasta salads are convenient to make because they can be made ahead. Fresh vegetable salads are a natural with grilled foods.

You will find new favorites among the salad combinations in this chapter, such as Mixed Greens, Avocado, and Mushroom Salad with Tangy Red Dressing (page 51); Orange, Cucumber, and Red Onion Salad with Lime-Cumin Dressing (page 54); Best Coleslaw (page 55); and New Potato Salad with Aioli (page 60).

ROMAINE, WATERCRESS, SHRIMP, AND AVOCADO SALAD WITH CREAMY TARRAGON DRESSING

Serves 4 to 6

Romaine is a hearty crisp lettuce that adds crunch to the salad. It holds up well when dressed and does not wilt like some of the other greens. Watercress has small dark green leaves that are slightly bitter. This can be served as a main-course salad or an accompaniment salad. The creamy dressing is seasoned with tarragon, an aromatic herb with a slight anise flavor often used in dressings and sauces. Tarragon vinegar can be found in gourmet markets.

In a large bowl, combine all salad ingredients and toss with enough dressing to coat.

6	to 8 cups torn romaine lettuce leaves
1	cup watercress leaves
1	avocado, peeled, pitted, and cut into bite-sized chunks
¼	cup chopped red onion
1	cup cooked small bay shrimp (optional)
	Creamy Tarragon Dressing (recipe follows)

CREAMY TARRAGON DRESSING

In a food processor or blender, combine all ingredients and process until well blended. Cover and refrigerate until ready to use.

Makes about 1 cup

¾	cup mayonnaise
¼	cup plain nonfat yogurt
2	green onions, including some tender green tops, coarsely chopped
1	garlic clove, coarsely chopped
2	tablespoons tarragon vinegar, or 2 tablespoons white wine vinegar plus ¼ teaspoon dried tarragon
1	teaspoon fresh lemon juice
¼	teaspoon salt

SPINACH SALAD WITH CUCUMBER, MUSHROOMS, AND FETA CHEESE WITH LEMON-DIJON VINAIGRETTE

Serves 6

This tossed salad with a light dressing and accented with feta cheese goes well with Lamb Chops with Crumb Topping (page 110).

In a large bowl, combine all salad ingredients and toss with enough dressing to coat.

6	to 8 cups baby spinach, stems removed if desired
3	ounces medium mushrooms, sliced
½	cup chopped red bell pepper
1	small cucumber, peeled, halved lengthwise, seeded, and sliced
¼	cup crumbled feta cheese
	Lemon-Dijon Vinaigrette (recipe follows)

LEMON-DIJON VINAIGRETTE

In a small bowl, whisk together all ingredients until slightly thickened and creamy.

Makes about ¾ cup

1	tablespoon Dijon mustard
3	tablespoons white wine vinegar
2	tablespoons fresh lemon juice
½	cup olive oil
1	garlic clove, minced
¼	teaspoon sugar
¼	teaspoon salt
	Freshly ground pepper to taste

SPINACH AND AVOCADO SALAD WITH DRIED CRANBERRIES, CANDIED WALNUTS, AND BLUE CHEESE

Serves 4 to 6

Spinach, which is painstaking to wash, has become easy to use in salads because it is now readily available in packages of prewashed, ready-to-use baby or mature spinach. The stems can be removed, if desired. Dressed up with dried cranberries and candied walnuts, this salad makes a good holiday salad to serve with turkey or ham.

In a large bowl, combine all salad ingredients and toss with enough dressing to coat.

8   cups baby spinach, stems removed if desired
2   avocados, peeled, pitted, and cut into bite-sized pieces
⅓   cup crumbled blue cheese
½   cup dried cranberries
½   cup Candied Walnuts (recipe on facing page)
    Raspberry Vinaigrette (recipe on facing page)

RASPBERRY VINAIGRETTE

In a small bowl, whisk together all ingredients.

Makes about ¾ cup

¼   cup raspberry vinegar
¼   cup olive oil
¼   cup vegetable oil
2   garlic cloves, minced
1   teaspoon sugar
1   teaspoon salt
     Freshly ground pepper to taste

CANDIED WALNUTS

In a small skillet over medium heat, melt butter and stir in brown sugar until sugar is dissolved. Add nuts and stir. Cook about 3 minutes, stirring occasionally. Dry on a piece of aluminum foil, separating the nuts so they won't stick together. Cool and use immediately or store in a covered container.

Makes about ½ cup

1   tablespoon butter
1   tablespoon firmly packed brown sugar
½   cup walnut or pecan halves

TOSSED GREEN SALAD WITH ITALIAN DRESSING

Serves 6 to 8

This basic tossed green salad is a agreat accompaniment to Ready Spaghetti (page 174) and other Italian-style dishes

In a large bowl, combine all salad ingredients and toss with enough dressing to coat.

8	to 10 cups mixed greens
1	tomato, cut into bite sized pieces and drained
6	green onions, including some tender green tops, sliced
5	or 6 mushrooms, sliced
1	cucumber, peeled, sliced lengthwise, seeded, and sliced (optional)
	Italian Dressing (recipe follows)

ITALIAN DRESSING

In a medium bowl, whisk together all ingredients.

Makes about ¾ cup

½	cup olive oil
¼	cup red wine vinegar
2	garlic cloves, minced
½	teaspoon dried basil
½	teaspoon dried oregano
¼	teaspoon dried thyme
¼	teaspoon salt
	Freshly ground pepper to taste

MIXED GREENS, AVOCADO, AND MUSHROOM SALAD WITH TANGY RED DRESSING

Serves 4 to 6

This will likely become one of your favorite year-round salads to accompany meats or poultry. The tangy dressing is outstanding and can be used on other green salads.

In a large bowl, combine all salad ingredients and toss with enough dressing to coat.

6	to 8 cups torn mixed salad greens
1	avocado, peeled, pitted, and sliced
3	ounces mushrooms, sliced
3	or 4 green onions, including some tender green tops, sliced
	Tangy Red Dressing (recipe follows)

TANGY RED DRESSING

In a small bowl, whisk together all ingredients. Whisk again before serving.

Makes about 1¼ cups

½	cup vegetable oil
½	cup ketchup
¼	cup cider vinegar
1	tablespoon fresh lemon juice
1	tablespoon honey
½	teaspoon Worcestershire sauce
⅛	teaspoon paprika
½	teaspoon salt
⅛	teaspoon freshly ground pepper

SPINACH WALDORF SALAD

Serves 4

Inspired by the famous Waldorf salad, this salad includes spinach, apples, nuts, and cheese and is tossed with a lemony mayonnaise. It is a good companion for seafood dishes.

Place apple in a large bowl and sprinkle with lemon juice. Add spinach, cheese, and nuts and toss with enough dressing to coat.

1	Granny Smith apple, unpeeled, cut into bite-sized pieces
	Juice of ½ lemon
6	cups baby spinach, stems removed if desired
4	ounces Cheddar cheese, cut into ½-inch cubes (about ½ cup)
¼	cup coarsely chopped walnuts
	Lemon Mayonnaise (recipe follows)

LEMON MAYONNAISE

In a small bowl, whisk together all ingredients. Cover and refrigerate until ready to use.

Makes about ½ cup

½	cup mayonnaise
2	tablespoons fresh lemon juice
1	teaspoon white wine vinegar
½	teaspoon sugar
¼	teaspoon salt

ROMAINE, ARUGULA, AND AVOCADO SALAD WITH CREAMY GARLIC-HERB BUTTERMILK DRESSING

Serves 8

Make this salad in the winter when garden-fresh vegetables are not available. Serve with Baked Mustard-Coated Chicken Breasts (page 121). Keep this favorite dressing on hand for other salads.

In a large salad bowl, combine all ingredients and toss with enough dressing to coat.

6	cups torn romaine lettuce leaves
3	cups torn arugula or spinach leaves
2	avocados, peeled, pitted, and sliced
½	cup sliced radishes
½	red onion, sliced and separated into rings
	Creamy Garlic-Herb Buttermilk Dressing (recipe follows)

CREAMY GARLIC-HERB BUTTERMILK DRESSING

In a food processor, combine all ingredients and process until blended. Cover and refrigerate until ready to use.

Makes about 1¾ cups

1	cup mayonnaise
¾	cup buttermilk
1	tablespoon white wine vinegar
2	or 3 garlic cloves, sliced
3	fresh parsley sprigs
1	green onion, including some tender green tops, coarsely chopped
¼	teaspoon dried marjoram
¼	teaspoon dried thyme
¼	teaspoon salt
	Freshly ground pepper to taste

ORANGE, CUCUMBER, AND RED ONION SALAD WITH LIME-CUMIN DRESSING

Serves 4

The tart flavor of lime provides a refreshing note to this salad. It adds a cooling touch when served with spicy food.

On a lettuce-lined platter, arrange orange, cucumber, and red onion slices. Drizzle on dressing.

Leaf lettuce leaves for lining the platter

3 oranges, peeled, white pith removed, and sliced

1 cucumber, peeled and sliced

1 small red onion, sliced

Lime-Cumin Dressing (recipe follows)

LIME-CUMIN DRESSING

In a small bowl, whisk together all ingredients.

Makes about ⅔ cup

Juice of 1 lime

1 tablespoon white wine vinegar

½ cup vegetable oil

1 tablespoon honey

¼ teaspoon dried oregano

½ teaspoon ground cumin

¼ teaspoon salt

Freshly ground pepper to taste

BEST COLESLAW

Serves 8

This crisp cabbage salad with a sweet-and-sour dressing gives just the right balance of flavors. Serve with Ribs with Really Good Barbecue Sauce (page 275) and Four-Bean Bake (page 201) for a traditional picnic supper.

In a large bowl, stir together onion and sugar. Let stand at room temperature 30 minutes. Add oil, vinegar, mayonnaise, and salt and whisk to blend. Cover and refrigerate.

Add cabbage to the bowl 1 to 2 hours before serving and mix well. Serve with a slotted spoon.

1   yellow onion, chopped
⅓   cup sugar
½   cup vegetable oil
½   cup cider vinegar
½   cup mayonnaise
1   teaspoon salt
1   large head green cabbage, shredded and chilled (5 to 6 cups)

CHOPPED GREEK SALAD

Serves 4

In this excellent salad, chopped vegetables are served on a bed of shredded lettuce and topped with feta cheese. Serve with Grilled Rosemary Lamb Chops (page 277).

In a large bowl, toss together all ingredients except lettuce and feta cheese. Cover and refrigerate 1 hour or longer to allow flavors to blend, stirring once. Divide lettuce among individual plates. Spoon vegetable mixture on top and sprinkle with feta cheese.

½ red or green bell pepper, seeded and chopped

½ cucumber, peeled, sliced lengthwise, seeded, and chopped

½ cup chopped red onion

1 garlic clove, finely chopped

1 plum (Roma) tomato, chopped

½ cup pitted Kalamata olives or black olives

1 teaspoon dried oregano

½ teaspoon salt

Freshly ground pepper to taste

2 tablespoons fresh lemon juice

2 tablespoons olive oil

3 cups shredded red lettuce leaves

¼ cup crumbled feta cheese

SUMMER SALAD BOWL
Serves 4 to 6

In this seasonal salad, a combination of red and yellow tomatoes and other garden vegetables are tossed with a flavorful Fresh Mixed Herb Dressing. Serve at a barbecue supper with Grilled Cabin Burgers (page 271).

Drain the tomato halves, cut side down, for about 5 minutes on paper towels.

In a large bowl, toss all ingredients with enough dressing to coat. Cover and refrigerate 30 minutes. Stir before serving.

1   cup cherry tomatoes, halved

1   medium red tomato, cut into 8 wedges

1   medium yellow tomato, cut into 8 wedges

1   cucumber, peeled, halved lengthwise, seeded, and sliced

1   bunch green onions, including some tender green tops, sliced

4   ounces mushrooms, quartered

     Fresh Mixed Herb Dressing (recipe follows)

FRESH MIXED HERB DRESSING

In a medium bowl, whisk together all ingredients.

Makes about ¾ cup

½   cup olive oil

¼   cup white wine vinegar

1   teaspoon Dijon mustard

1   tablespoon finely chopped mixed fresh herbs or ¾ teaspoon dried mixed herbs

1   tablespoon chopped fresh chives

1   tablespoon chopped fresh parsley

¼   teaspoon salt

     Freshly ground pepper to taste

GREEN BEANS WITH TOASTED ALMONDS AND BLUE CHEESE SALAD

Serves 4

Take this summer salad to a family picnic or potluck supper. Make ahead several hours to allow flavors to mellow and chill thoroughly.

In a medium saucepan over high heat, bring just enough water to cover beans to a boil. Add beans and cook, uncovered, until tender-crisp, about 3 minutes. Drain under cold water and place in a bowl.

In a small bowl, whisk together oil, vinegar, lemon juice, mustard, and salt and pour over beans. Cover and refrigerate several hours to allow flavors to blend. Transfer to a platter and sprinkle with pepper, blue cheese, and almonds just before serving.

1   pound fresh green beans, trimmed
3   tablespoons olive oil
1   tablespoon white wine vinegar
1   tablespoon fresh lemon juice
1   teaspoon Dijon mustard
¼   teaspoon salt
     Freshly ground pepper to taste
½   cup crumbled blue cheese
3   tablespoons sliced almonds, toasted (see Note, page 33)

POTATO SALAD EVERYONE LOVES
Serves 6

This potato salad combines potatoes, eggs, celery, and green onions with a light, creamy dill dressing. Include this salad on a supper menu of Favorite Barbecued Chicken (page 283) and fresh corn on the cob.

In a saucepan over medium-high heat, bring just enough lightly salted water to cover potatoes to a boil. Add potatoes, reduce heat to medium, and cook, covered, until tender, about 20 minutes. Drain under cold water. When cool enough to handle, slice and place in a large bowl with eggs, celery, parsley, and green onions. Toss with enough dressing to coat, cover, and refrigerate 3 to 4 hours to allow flavors to blend.

4   russet potatoes (1½ to 2 pounds), peeled and halved

3   hard-cooked eggs, peeled and chopped

½   cup chopped celery

2   tablespoons chopped fresh parsley

½   cup sliced green onions, including some tender green tops

Creamy Dill Dressing (page 39)

NEW POTATO SALAD WITH AIOLI

Serves 8

This potato salad is combined with crunchy vegetables and a garlicky may-onnaise that make the salad distinctive. Aioli originated in southern France and is popular as an accompaniment for fish, meats, and vegetables and in sandwiches and salads.

In a large saucepan over high heat, bring just enough lightly salted water to cover potatoes to a boil. Add potatoes, reduce heat to medium, and cook, covered, until tender, about 20 minutes. Drain under cold water. When cool enough to handle, quarter, then slice and place in a large bowl. Toss with vinegar. Add celery, bell pepper, radishes, green onions, and parsley and toss with Aioli. Season with salt and pepper. Cover and refrigerate several hours to allow flavors to blend.

8	to 10 unpeeled medium red-skinned new potatoes (about 2 pounds), scrubbed and halved
2	tablespoons white wine vinegar
1	cup chopped celery
¾	cup chopped red bell pepper
½	cup sliced red radishes
4	green onions, including some tender green tops, sliced
¼	cup chopped fresh parsley
	Aioli (recipe follows)
	Salt and freshly ground pepper to taste

AIOLI

In a medium bowl, whisk together all ingredi-ents. Cover and refrigerate until ready to use.

Makes about 1 cup

¾	cup mayonnaise
1	teaspoon Dijon mustard
3	or 4 large garlic cloves, minced
½	teaspoon salt

EXOTIC FRUIT SALAD
Serves 4

This elegant salad of luscious, juicy fruit topped with a unique Peanut Butter Dressing goes well with Grilled Honey-Mustard Pork Tenderloin (page 274).

Arrange fruit on a platter and garnish with mint leaves. Pass dressing in a small pitcher.

6	fresh pineapple slices
1	mango or papaya, peeled and sliced
½	cantaloupe, peeled and sliced
1	or 2 kiwi fruits, peeled and sliced
	Fresh mint leaves for garnish
	Peanut Butter Dressing (recipe follows)

PEANUT BUTTER DRESSING

In a food processor or blender, combine peanut butter, pineapple juice, and mint leaves. With motor running, slowly add oil and process until smooth.

Makes about 1 cup

2	tablespoons chunky peanut butter
¼	cup pineapple juice
2	fresh mint leaves, torn
⅓	cup vegetable oil

BLUEBERRY-MELON BOWL WITH HONEY-YOGURT DRESSING

Serves 6

Don't let summer pass you by without making this healthful, seasonal salad served with a light dressing. This is a refreshing accompaniment to Grilled Halibut Steaks Wrapped in Bacon (page 289).

In a large bowl, toss together all the melons. Cover and refrigerate several hours to allow melons to release water and flavors to blend. Drain, add blueberries, and toss lightly. Garnish with mint leaves. Pass dressing in a small pitcher.

½   cantaloupe, cut into 1-inch chunks
½   honeydew melon, cut into 1-inch chunks
2   cups 1-inch watermelon chunks
1   cup blueberries, rinsed, drained, and dried
    Fresh mint leaves for garnish
    Honey-Yogurt Dressing (recipe follows)

HONEY-YOGURT DRESSING

In a bowl, whisk together all ingredients. Cover and refrigerate until ready to use.

Makes about ¾ cup

¾   cup plain nonfat yogurt
1   tablespoon honey
¼   teaspoon ground cinnamon

PASTA AND VEGETABLE SALAD WITH CREAMY DILL DRESSING

Serves 6

Here is a side salad that goes well with Grilled Marinated Beef Roast (page 264). Other vegetables may be used depending on the season. Take advantage of new arrivals at the farmers' market.

Drain the tomato halves, cut side down, for 5 minutes on paper towels. In a large bowl, toss pasta with oil to keep pasta from sticking together. Cover and refrigerate 1 hour. Add remaining ingredients except basil leaves to the pasta and toss with enough dressing to coat. Cover and chill several hours to allow flavors to blend. Garnish with basil leaves before serving.

1 cup cherry tomatoes, halved

8 ounces (2 ½ cups) rotini or fusilli, cooked according to package directions and drained

1 tablespoon vegetable oil

½ cup chopped red bell pepper

4 green onions, including some tender green tops, sliced

2 celery stalks, chopped

2 or 3 mushrooms, chopped

½ cup pitted black olives

Creamy Dill Dressing (page 39)

Fresh basil leaves for garnish

SANDWICHES

CHAPTER 4

SUBSTANTIAL MAIN-COURSE SELECTIONS

For a quick supper, you can always rely on a hearty, satisfying supper sandwich. With the new artisan breads, exciting fillings, and gourmet spreads, today's sandwiches take on elegance and new interest.

This chapter features some cold sandwiches and others that are toasted—you can use a sandwich maker or panini, the oven, or a griddle or skillet for toasting. Panini are state-of-the-art sandwich presses with adjustable lids that accommodate sky-high sandwiches. They can be somewhat expensive, but produce beautiful, grill-marked toasted sandwiches with a minimum of fuss.

Enjoy a simple supper with a Grilled Steak Hero Sandwich (page 66), Sloppy Joes (page 68), a Reuben Supper Sandwich (page 86), Crab on a Muffin (page 80), Warm Tuna Rolls (page 82), or Turkey Breast with Roasted Red Pepper in Focaccia (page 74), and turn the pages for other appealing combinations.

GRILLED STEAK HERO SANDWICH

Serves 4

This hearty sandwich with a garlicky horseradish mayonnaise will appeal to those who like bold flavors. Serve this sandwich with the Potato Salad Everyone Loves (page 59) for an easy patio supper. The steak can also be broiled.

Preheat grill. Lightly brush steak with vegetable oil on both sides and grill over high heat until medium-rare, 12 to 15 minutes, or to desired doneness, turning once. Transfer to a cutting board and cut on the diagonal across the grain into thin (⅛- to ¼-inch) strips. Lightly spread cut sides of each roll with Garlicky Horseradish Mayonnaise. Layer steak strips, onion slices, and a lettuce leaf on bottom half of each roll. Replace tops of rolls. Garnish the plate with radishes.

1   large top sirloin steak, ¾ inch thick (about 1 pound)
    Vegetable oil for brushing
4   French hero rolls, split lengthwise and warmed (see Note)
    Garlicky Horseradish Mayonnaise (recipe follows)
½   red onion, thinly sliced
4   large red leaf lettuce leaves
    Red radishes for garnish

NOTE: To warm rolls, wrap in foil and heat in 350ºF oven for 10 to 15 minutes.

GARLICKY HORSERADISH MAYONNAISE

Horseradish is an ancient herb grown mainly for the white pungent root. Fresh horseradish should be kept in the refrigerator and peeled just before using. It is very hot, so use caution. Prepared horseradish is available in jars.

In a bowl, whisk together all ingredients. Cover and refrigerate until ready to use.

Makes about ¾ cup

½   cup mayonnaise
3   garlic cloves, minced
1   teaspoon grated fresh horseradish or 2 tablespoons prepared horseradish
¼   teaspoon dry mustard
¼   teaspoon salt
    Freshly ground pepper to taste

HOT BARBECUED BEEF SANDWICH
Serves 4

For a cozy supper on a cold winter night, serve these barbe-cued sandwiches with Best Coleslaw (page 55) and baked beans. Leftover pork can be used instead of beef.

Brush cut side of buns with warm barbecue sauce. Dip beef slices into barbecue sauce and place in buns. Add more sauce on top and serve immediately.

4   hamburger buns, split and warmed (see Note, facing page)

    Easy Barbecue Sauce (recipe follows) or purchased barbecue sauce, warmed

¾   to 1 pound thinly sliced roast beef

EASY BARBECUE SAUCE

In a medium saucepan over medium heat, combine all ingredients and simmer 5 minutes.

Makes about 1 cup

¾   cup ketchup

¼   cup chili sauce

½   cup water

2   teaspoons Worcestershire sauce

2   teaspoons cider vinegar

1   tablespoon honey

SLOPPY JOES
Serves 4

Hamburger buns are filled with cooked ground beef, onions, celery, and green bell pepper in a snappy tomato sauce. This is a fun, easy sandwich the whole family will enjoy. The name is obvious, they are messy to eat!

In a medium skillet over medium heat, combine beef, onion, celery, garlic, and bell pepper and sauté, breaking up meat with a spoon, until beef is browned and vegetables are tender, about 10 minutes, adding a little oil if needed. Add tomato sauce, chili sauce, Worcestershire sauce, Tabasco, salt, and pepper and simmer 5 minutes to blend flavors. Divide mixture evenly on hamburger buns and serve immediately.

1	pound ground beef
½	cup chopped yellow onion
½	cup chopped celery
2	garlic cloves, minced
½	cup diced green bell pepper
	Vegetable oil, as needed
½	cup tomato sauce
1	tablespoon chili sauce
1	tablespoon Worcestershire sauce
2	or 3 drops Tabasco sauce
¼	teaspoon salt
	Freshly ground pepper to taste
4	large hamburger buns, split and warmed (see Note, page 66)

MEXICAN HAMBURGER PATTIES
Serves 4

For a speedy midweek meal, serve these zippy broiled patties in warm buns, topped with cheese, salsa, avocado, and onion slices. Serve with a basket of tortilla chips alongside.

Preheat broiler. In a medium bowl, mix together beef, salt, and pepper. Form into 4 patties. Broil 4 inches from heat until meat is no longer pink in the center, about 4 minutes on each side. Top with cheese slices and broil until cheese is melted, about 30 seconds longer. Spread mayonnaise on each half of buns. Layer a beef patty, onions, avocado slices, and a lettuce leaf on each bun bottom, then place remaining buns on top. Serve immediately. Pass salsa in a bowl, if desired.

1¼ pounds ground beef

½ teaspoon salt

Freshly ground pepper to taste

4 slices pepper Jack cheese

1 to 2 tablespoons mayonnaise

4 hamburger buns, split and warmed (see Note, page 66)

½ red onion, sliced

1 avocado, peeled, pitted, and sliced

4 large lettuce leaves

Fresh Tomato Salsa (page 71) or good-quality purchased salsa for serving (optional)

TURKEY TACOS

Serves 4

The Mexican taco can be infinitely adapted to virtually any favorite ingredient, including beef, ground turkey, chicken, sausage, or seafood, with assorted toppings. They are fun and easy for a casual supper.

Warm the tortillas (see Note). Meanwhile, in a large nonstick skillet over medium heat, warm oil. Add turkey and sauté, breaking up meat with a spoon, until meat is browned, about 5 minutes. Add salsa and seasonings and mix well. In a medium saucepan over low heat, combine beans and butter and cook, stirring occasionally, until warmed through.

To assemble, cover a tortilla with a light coating of bean mixture. Add about 2 tablespoons meat mixture in a strip down the center. Add a spoonful of salsa and sour cream, a few chopped green onions, tomatoes, cheese, lettuce, and other toppings of your choice. Fold in half and serve immediately. Repeat with remaining tortillas and filling.

NOTE: To warm tortillas, wrap in damp paper towels and warm in the microwave oven for 30 seconds or in a preheated 350°F oven for 10 minutes.

8   soft corn tortillas or purchased crisp folded taco shells

2   teaspoons vegetable oil

1¼ pounds ground turkey

¼   cup Fresh Tomato Salsa (recipe on facing page) or good-quality purchased tomato salsa, slightly drained

1   teaspoon chili powder

¼   teaspoon ground cumin

½   teaspoon salt
    Freshly ground pepper to taste

3   or 4 drops Tabasco sauce

1   can (16 ounces) refried beans, preferably vegetarian

1   tablespoon butter

TOPPINGS

Fresh Tomato Salsa

Sour cream

Chopped green onions

Chopped tomatoes

Grated Cheddar cheese

Shredded lettuce

Chopped avocados (optional)

Chopped olives (optional)

FRESH TOMATO SALSA

Homemade salsa is best eaten the same day as prepared.

In a medium bowl, stir together all ingredients. Cover and let stand at room temperature at least 1 hour to allow flavors to blend, then cover and store in refrigerator until ready to use. Drain, if necessary, before using.

Makes about 3 cups

4   tomatoes, seeded (see Note, page 179), chopped, and drained
½   cup diced green bell pepper (optional)
½   cup chopped yellow onion
1   tablespoon seeded and minced jalapeño pepper, or 1 tablespoon diced canned chiles, drained
2   garlic cloves, minced
    Juice of 1 small lime
1   tablespoon olive oil
¼   cup chopped fresh cilantro or parsley
1   tablespoon chopped fresh oregano or ¾ teaspoon dried oregano
½   teaspoon salt
    Freshly ground pepper to taste

BEEF AND BEAN BURRITOS

Serves 4

Beans are a traditional ingredient in burritos, combined with meats or poultry and cheese in a folded tortilla. Kids are usually big burrito fans, although you may want to reduce the spices for young taste buds.

Warm the tortillas (see Note, page 70). Meanwhile, in a medium skillet over medium heat, combine beef, onion, and garlic and sauté, breaking up meat with a spoon, until meat is browned and vegetables are tender, 6 to 7 minutes, adding a little oil if needed. Season with chili powder, cumin, salt, and pepper. Stir in beans, salsa, and cilantro and simmer about 5 minutes longer.

To assemble, spoon some filling on the lower one-third of a tortilla and sprinkle with about 1 tablespoon cheese. Fold the bottom edge up halfway, pressing gently over filling. Fold over the sides to completely cover the filling and finish rolling. Repeat with remaining tortillas and filling. Serve with sour cream, salsa, and avocado slices.

8	10-inch flour tortillas
½	pound ground beef
1	cup chopped yellow onion
1	garlic clove, minced
	Vegetable oil, as needed
½	teaspoon chili powder
¼	teaspoon ground cumin
¼	teaspoon salt
	Freshly ground pepper to taste
1	can (15 ounces) pinto or black beans, drained and rinsed
½	cup Fresh Tomato Salsa (page 71) or good-quality purchased tomato salsa
3	tablespoons chopped fresh cilantro or parsley
¾	cup grated Monterey Jack cheese
	Sour cream, additional salsa, and sliced avocado for serving

CONEY ISLAND HOT DOGS
Serves 4 to 6

High time to revive the Coney Island hot dog sandwich that originated in Coney Island, New York, in the early days of that beloved amusement park and summer destination. These hot dogs are covered with a spicy, meaty tomato sauce. They are messy to eat but fun; keeping forks handy is recommended.

In a skillet over medium heat, combine beef, onion, and garlic, and sauté, breaking up meat with a spoon, until meat is browned and vegetables are tender, 6 to 7 minutes, adding a little oil if needed. Add tomato purée and seasonings. Reduce heat to medium-low and simmer, uncovered, 10 minutes. In a medium saucepan over medium-high heat, cook hot dogs in water until heated through, about 5 minutes.

To assemble, place hot dogs in buns. Add enough sauce to cover the hot dogs generously.

CONEY ISLAND MEAT SAUCE

½   pound ground beef

1   cup chopped yellow onion

1   garlic clove, minced

    Vegetable oil, as needed

1   can (10¾ ounces) tomato purée

1   teaspoon chili powder

¼   teaspoon dry mustard

½   teaspoon salt

    Freshly ground pepper to taste

6   hot dogs, sliced lengthwise but kept intact

6   hot dog buns, split and warmed (see Note, page 66)

VARIATION: Omit sautéing onions with beef and use chopped raw onions on top of the meat sauce.

TURKEY BREAST WITH ROASTED RED BELL PEPPER IN FOCACCIA

Serves 4

Use leftover turkey breast or purchased turkey breast in this sandwich. Focaccia is a large, flat, round Italian bread brushed with olive oil, salt, and sometimes herbs. It can be eaten as a side bread or used as a base for sandwiches. It comes prebaked and can be purchased at well-stocked supermarkets, Italian markets, and specialty bakeries.

Preheat oven to 400°F. Wrap focaccia in aluminum foil and warm in the oven, about 6 minutes. Remove from oven and foil and cut in half, then split horizontally. In a small bowl, mix together mayonnaise and garlic. Spread mayonnaise mixture evenly on cut sides of two focaccia quarters. Layer half the turkey slices, roasted red bell pepper strips, onion rings, and lettuce leaves on each dressed piece. Top with the remaining focaccia pieces. Cut each half in half again to serve.

1   focaccia (16 ounces)

½   cup mayonnaise

2   garlic cloves, minced

½   pound sliced roasted turkey breast

1   roasted red bell pepper (see Note), cut into strips, or 1 jar (7 ounces) roasted red bell peppers, rinsed, drained, patted dry, and cut into strips

2   slices red onion, separated into rings

4   green leaf lettuce leaves

NOTE: To roast a bell pepper, preheat broiler. Halve pepper lengthwise and remove seeds and ribs. Make several 1-inch slits in each pepper half. Place, skin side up, on an aluminum foil–lined baking sheet. Press pepper halves down with the palm of your hand to flatten. Broil 4 inches from the heat until skin is charred, about 10 minutes. Remove from broiler, fold foil tightly over pepper, and let it steam for 10 to 15 minutes. Unwrap pepper and peel off skin. A whole pepper can also be roasted over a gas flame by spearing it with a long-handled fork and turning as it becomes charred, or placed on a grill and turned with tongs.

TOASTED CHICKEN AND SWISS CHEESE SANDWICH WITH ALMONDS

Serves 4

In this toasted sandwich, Swiss cheese melts over tender chicken, with nuts added for flavor and crunch.

Preheat sandwich maker. Spread bread slices on one side with mayonnaise. Divide chicken among 4 slices of bread and sprinkle with almonds. Add a slice of cheese and a lettuce leaf. Top with remaining bread slices and brush tops with butter. Brush bottom of sandwich maker with butter. Add 2 sandwiches, close lid, and cook until golden brown, about 3 minutes. Repeat to make 2 remaining sandwiches. Cut in half to serve.

8	slices sourdough bread
1	tablespoon mayonnaise
2	cups diced cooked chicken breast (see Note, page 30)
¼	cup sliced almonds, toasted (see Note, page 33)
4	slices Swiss cheese
4	large green leaf lettuce leaves
	Melted butter for brushing

GRILLED CHICKEN SANDWICH WITH ROASTED RED BELL PEPPER AIOLI

Serves 4

Marinated grilled chicken is enhanced with Roasted Red Bell Pepper Aioli in this filling sandwich. Make the aioli several hours ahead to allow the flavors to blend. Serve with Potato Salad Everyone Loves (page 59) for a summer supper.

In a large shallow bowl, combine marinade ingredients. Add chicken breasts and turn to coat. Cover and marinate 1 hour in the refrigerator. Bring to room temperature before grilling.

Preheat grill. Remove chicken breasts from marinade and discard marinade. Grill over medium heat until chicken is no longer pink in the center, 6 to 8 minutes on each side, turning once. While the chicken cooks, brush bread with oil on both sides. Place bread on grill and toast 1 to 2 minutes, turning once.

To assemble, spread toasted bread generously with aioli. Place each chicken breast between 2 bread slices. Cut each sandwich in half to serve.

MARINADE

2   tablespoons olive oil
2   tablespoons fresh lemon juice
½   teaspoon dried thyme
¼   teaspoon salt
    Freshly ground pepper to taste

4   boned and skinned chicken breast halves (6 to 8 ounces each)
8   slices French bread
    Vegetable oil for brushing
    Roasted Red Bell Pepper Aioli (page 165)

CHICKEN, AVOCADO, AND RED BELL PEPPER WRAP

Serves 4

Wraps are fun to make and easy to eat. Tortillas are used instead of bread. They can be filled with a variety of fillings and served as a main course. For variety, look for flavored tortillas.

In a medium bowl, combine all ingredients except tortillas. Lay tortillas on a flat surface. Spoon one-fourth of the chicken mixture across the lower third of a tortilla. Fold the bottom edge up halfway, pressing gently over filling. Fold over the sides to completely cover filling and finish rolling. Repeat with remaining tortillas and filling.

1½ cups shredded or chopped cooked chicken breast (see Note, page 30)

1 avocado, peeled, pitted, and cut into bite-sized pieces

1 roasted red bell pepper (see Note, page 74), cut into strips, or 1 jar (7 ounces) roasted red bell peppers, rinsed, drained and patted dry; cut into strips

¼ cup mayonnaise

1 teaspoon Dijon mustard

1 teaspoon fresh lemon juice

¼ teaspoon salt

4 large flour tortillas, warmed (see Note, page 70)

THE CLASSIC CLUB

Serves 4

Here is the famous club sandwich without the third slice of bread (who needs it?). Layers of sliced turkey breast, tomato, crisp bacon, lettuce, and mayonnaise on toasted bread make up this version.

Spread mayonnaise on bread slices. Top each of 4 bread slices with turkey, tomato slices, bacon, and a lettuce leaf. Place remaining bread slices on top. Cut each sandwich in half and serve with potato chips.

¼ cup mayonnaise

8 slices firm white bread, crusts removed (optional) and lightly toasted

½ pound sliced roasted turkey breast

2 tomatoes, sliced

8 thick bacon slices, cooked until crisp and drained

4 large lettuce leaves

Potato chips for serving

TURKEY PESTO PANINI
Serves 4

While out of town on a book-signing trip, I ordered this sandwich at a cozy little deli. It was so good, I adapted it for this book. Panini is Italian for "roll." It is also the name of a type of sandwich-toasting press with an adjustable lid that will accommodate thick sandwiches.

Preheat panini press or other sandwich maker. Spread 4 bread slices with pesto on one side and the other 4 with mayonnaise. Divide remaining sandwich ingredients (except butter) equally among mayonnaise-dressed bread slices. Top with remaining bread slices, pesto side down, and brush tops with butter. Brush bottom of panini press with butter. Add 2 sandwiches, close lid, and cook until lightly browned and cheese is melted, about 5 minutes. Repeat to make remaining 2 sandwiches. Cut each sandwich in half to serve.

8   slices crusty Italian bread
¼   cup Basil Pesto (page 190)
1   to 2 tablespoons mayonnaise
¾   pound thinly sliced roasted turkey breast
1   tomato, thinly sliced
½   red onion, thinly sliced
4   slices Gouda cheese
     Melted butter for brushing

CRAB ON A MUFFIN

Serves 4

Make these open-faced sandwiches during peak crab season for a "melt in your mouth" experience. Serve with fresh winter fruit, such as pears and apples.

Preheat broiler. In a medium bowl, combine cream cheese, mayonnaise, mustard, Worcestershire sauce, and Tabasco and blend. Add crab and mix well. Spread mixture on each muffin half. Top each with tomato slices, cheese, and bacon. Arrange on a baking sheet and broil until cheese is bubbly and bacon is crisp, 3 to 4 minutes.

4	ounces cream cheese, at room temperature
3	tablespoons mayonnaise
½	teaspoon dry mustard
½	teaspoon Worcestershire sauce
2	or 3 drops Tabasco sauce
6	ounces lump crabmeat, picked over and flaked
4	English muffins, split and lightly toasted
2	tomatoes, thinly sliced
8	slices Cheddar cheese
4	slices bacon, halved and partially cooked (see Note)

NOTE: To partially cook bacon, place on a paper plate lined with several layers of paper towels. Cover with 2 paper towels and microwave until just translucent, about 1 minute. Alternatively, fry in a small skillet over medium heat for 3 to 4 minutes.

SHRIMP MELT

Serves 4

These open-faced muffins topped with a mixture of shrimp, cheese, and mayonnaise are quick and easy, with a touch of luxury for a light supper.

Preheat broiler. Combine shrimp, mayonnaise, chili sauce, and cheese. Place muffins on a baking sheet, cut side down. Broil 4 inches from the heat for 1 minute. Turn and spread each with seafood mixture. Broil until bubbly but not browned, 1½ to 2 minutes longer. Watch carefully to prevent burning.

¾ pound cooked small bay shrimp
3 tablespoons mayonnaise
2 tablespoons chili sauce
1 cup grated Monterey Jack cheese
4 English muffins, split

WARM TUNA ROLLS

Serves 4

We always keep canned tuna on hand as a staple at our cabin on the McKenzie River, because hungry boating and rafting friends often stop by for a snack. Everyone likes these warmed rolls filled with tuna, crunchy celery, green onion, and pickle, and topped with melted cheese.

Preheat oven to 350°F. Remove some of the soft bread in the center of top and bottom of rolls. Discard or save for bread crumbs.

In a medium bowl, combine remaining ingredients except cheese. Divide tuna filling among bottoms of rolls. Add cheese and replace tops of rolls. Wrap in foil and bake until heated through and cheese is melted, about 15 minutes.

4	sesame-seed Kaiser rolls, split lengthwise
2	cans (6½ ounces each) solid white tuna packed in water, drained
⅓	cup chopped celery
¼	cup sliced green onions, including some tender green tops
1	sweet pickle, chopped
⅓ to ½	cup mayonnaise
1	tablespoon Dijon mustard
½	teaspoon dried dill
2	teaspoons fresh lemon juice
4	ounces Cheddar cheese, thinly sliced to fit the rolls

TUNA IN PITA BREAD

Serves 4

Pita, also called pocket bread, is a Middle Eastern flat bread. Each individual round loaf, when cut in half and split open, makes a pocket that is handily stuffed with any filling you please. Here is a choice of two tuna fillings, or feel free to create your own.

Preheat oven to 350°F. In a medium bowl, mix together all ingredients except pita bread. Open pita halves and divide tuna mixture among them. Wrap each pita in aluminum foil and bake until warmed through, about 15 minutes.

FILLING NUMBER 1

2   cans (6½ ounces each) solid white tuna packed in oil, drained

½   cup mayonnaise

¼   cup chopped celery

¼   teaspoon curry powder (optional)

4   green onions, including some tender green tops, sliced

4   pimiento-stuffed green olives, chopped

FILLING NUMBER 2

2   cans (6½ ounces each) solid white tuna packed in oil, drained

½   cup mayonnaise

1   tablespoon capers, drained

2   tablespoons chopped red onion

1   teaspoon fresh lemon juice

4   small pita breads, halved and split

SMOKED SALMON AND WASABI CREAM CHEESE SANDWICH

Serves 4

Serve this open-faced sandwich with a refreshing Exotic Fruit Salad (page 61) for a fast supper with an Eastern flair. This also makes a good hors d'oeuvre spread on water crackers. Wasabi is the Japanese version of horseradish, used to make a sharp and pungent condiment. It is available in Asian and well-stocked supermarkets, in convenient premixed paste form or a powdered version that you mix with water to make a paste to use as needed.

In a medium bowl, combine cream cheese and wasabi and mix until blended. Add salmon and lemon juice and mix well. Spread salmon mixture on baguette slices. Top each with a cucumber slice and place an olive slice in the middle of the cucumber.

4	ounces light cream cheese, at room temperature
1	teaspoon wasabi paste, or more to taste
3	ounces smoked salmon, skin removed, flaked
1	teaspoon fresh lemon juice
8	baguette slices
½	cucumber, peeled and sliced
4	pimiento-stuffed olives, sliced

FILLED HAM AND CHEESE ROLLS
Serves 6

Two dressed-up fillings are layered in this appetizing sandwich that makes a complete meal. These sandwiches can be made ahead, wrapped in aluminum foil, and then heated just before serving.

Preheat oven to 350°F. Spread cut sides of rolls lightly with mayonnaise. On bottom half of the rolls, spread a layer of ham filling, then a layer of cheese filling. Replace tops of rolls. Wrap sandwiches in aluminum foil and bake until warmed through, 15 to 20 minutes.

6   crusty sourdough sandwich rolls, split lengthwise
1   to 2 tablespoons mayonnaise
    Ham Filling (recipe follows)
    Cheese Filling (recipe follows)

HAM FILLING

In a medium bowl, combine all ingredients.

Makes about 2 cups

2   cups chopped or ground cooked ham
2   tablespoons finely chopped sweet pickle
3   tablespoons mayonnaise
2   tablespoons sweet pickle juice
1   teaspoon prepared mustard

CHEESE FILLING

In a medium bowl, combine all ingredients.

Makes about 2 cups

2   cups grated Cheddar cheese
6   green onions, including some tender green tops, thinly sliced
2   tablespoons chopped black olives
3   tablespoons mayonnaise

REUBEN SUPPER SANDWICH

Serves 4

Reuben sandwiches are usually made with sauerkraut, corned beef, and Swiss cheese. In this variation, crisp coleslaw and pastrami are called for, and the sandwich is toasted on a griddle. You'll love the combination.

Preheat griddle. Place one-fourth of the pastrami slices on each of 4 pieces of the bread. Spread about ⅓ cup of slaw on top of each. Add a cheese slice to each and top with remaining bread slices. Brush tops of sandwich and griddle with butter. Place sandwiches on the griddle and toast until golden-brown and cheese is melted, about 2 minutes on each side. Serve with remaining slaw.

4   ounces thinly sliced pastrami
8   slices rye or pumpernickel bread
     Russian Slaw (recipe follows)
4   ounces thinly sliced Swiss cheese
     Melted butter for brushing

RUSSIAN SLAW

Make several hours ahead.

Place cabbage in a large bowl. In a medium bowl, combine mayonnaise, chili sauce, relish, salt, pepper, and Tabasco. Add to cabbage and mix well.

Makes about 4 cups

½   head green cabbage, shredded (about 4 cups)
½   cup mayonnaise
2   tablespoons chili sauce
1   tablespoon sweet pickle relish or 1 sweet pickle finely diced
¼   teaspoon salt
     Freshly ground pepper to taste
2   or 3 drops Tabasco sauce

BROILED PORTOBELLO AND TOMATO SANDWICH

Serves 4

Portobello mushrooms are so meaty in texture and rich in flavor, they are often used as a meat substitute. Broiling or grilling intensifies their flavor.

Preheat broiler. Brush both sides of mushrooms with olive oil. Season with salt and pepper. Broil until tender, about 5 minutes on each side. Spread mayonnaise on each half of buns. Layer a mushroom, tomato slices, onion, and a lettuce leaf on each bottom bun, then place remaining buns on top.

4   portobello mushrooms, cleaned with a
    damp paper towel and stems removed
¼   cup olive oil
    Salt and freshly ground pepper to taste
1   tablespoon mayonnaise
4   large hamburger buns, split and warmed
    (see Note, page 66)
1   tomato, thinly sliced
½   sweet white onion, thinly sliced
4   large lettuce leaves

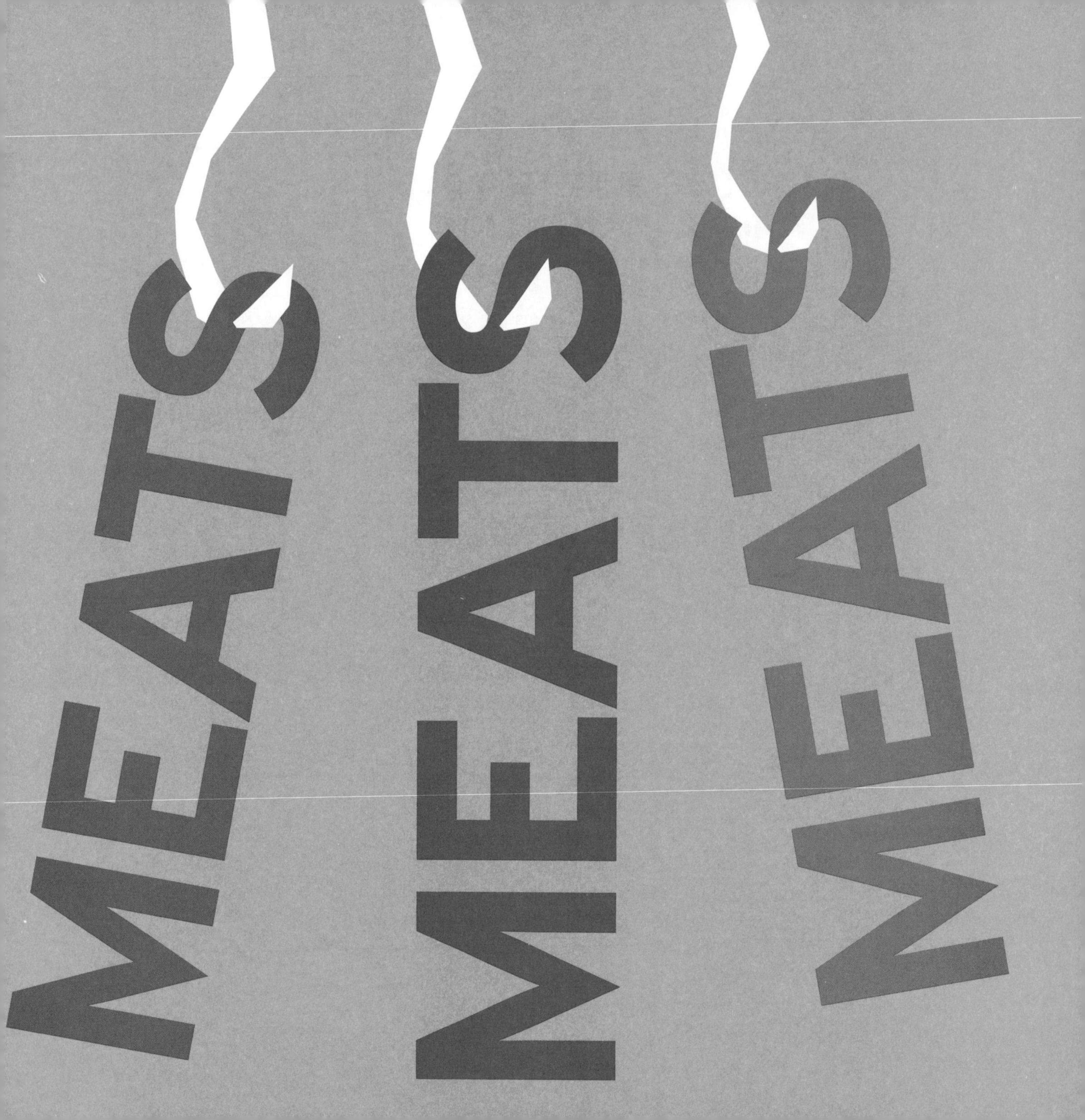
MEATS
MEATS
MEATS

CHAPTER 5

STANDBY ENTRÉES FEATURING BEEF, LAMB, AND PORK

Meats are a mainstay and a popular choice for many supper main courses. They are satisfying, full of hearty flavor, and, of course, a good source of protein.

In most supermarkets, good-quality meat is available prepackaged and labeled with weight, price per pound, total price, and name of the cut. This is a quick and easy way to buy meats. For specialty cuts and all-natural options, seek out meat markets and supermarkets that offer butcher service and feature these meats. After purchase, store meat lightly wrapped in the refrigerator and use as soon as possible.

The recipes in this chapter include a variety of meats with easy-to-follow directions. Some are basic and homey for quick family suppers; others are dressed up with easy sauces and toppings to serve for company. Many of the casseroles include ground beef, but ground turkey or chicken can be substituted, if preferred.

In this chapter, you will find a wide selection of meat entrées such as Steak Topped with Blue Cheese (page 90), Easy Flank Steak in a Tomato-Beer Marinade (page 93), Hamburger Stroganoff (page 99), Pork Chops with Sour Cream–Dill Sauce (page 102), Salsa Pork Chops (page 103), and Lamb Chops with Crumb Topping (page 110).

STEAK TOPPED WITH BLUE CHEESE

Serves 4

New York steaks are one of the most popular cuts of beef. They are tender, juicy, and full of flavor. The blue cheese adds a distinctive touch and makes these steaks even more special. Serve with Garlic Roasted Vegetables (page 227) and Mixed Greens, Avocado, and Mushroom Salad with Tangy Red Dressing (page 51).

Preheat broiler. Brush steaks with oil and season with salt and pepper. Place steaks on broiler pan. Broil 4 inches from heat for 5 minutes. Turn with tongs and broil 5 to 6 minutes longer for medium-rare. Spread 1 teaspoon blue cheese on each steak and broil until cheese starts to melt, about 30 seconds longer. Serve immediately.

4 New York steaks (8 to 10 ounces each)
Vegetable oil for brushing
Salt and freshly ground pepper to taste
4 teaspoons crumbled blue cheese

BROILED STEAK WITH HERB BUTTER

Serves 4

Fabulous and fast, this steak is quickly broiled to taste, then topped with a mouth-watering herb-seasoned butter. Serve with Lemony Green Beans with Toasted Pine Nuts (page 206).

Preheat broiler. Place steaks on broiler pan. Broil 4 inches from heat for 5 minutes. Turn with tongs and broil 5 to 6 minutes longer for medium-rare. Spread on Herb Butter and broil 1 minute longer.

4   top sirloin steaks (about 8 ounces each)
    Herb Butter (recipe follows)

HERB BUTTER

In a small bowl, mix together all ingredients.

Makes about ⅓ cup

¼   cup (½ stick) butter, at room temperature
¼   teaspoon salt
¼   teaspoon dried marjoram
¼   teaspoon dried basil
¼   teaspoon dried thyme
¼   teaspoon ground mustard
¼   teaspoon freshly ground pepper
1   tablespoon chopped fresh chives

BEEF IN TOMATO-WINE SAUCE

Serves 4 to 6

For easy supper preparation, make this recipe ahead and bake it later. Cook the rice side dish just before serving. Try the Mixed Greens, Avocado, and Mushroom Salad with Tangy Red Dressing (page 51) as an accompaniment.

Preheat oven to 350°F. On a piece of waxed paper, combine flour, salt, and pepper. Add beef cubes and toss to coat.

In a Dutch oven over medium-high heat, warm oil. Add beef, onion, and garlic and sauté until meat is lightly browned and onions are tender, 6 to 7 minutes. Stir in paprika. Stir in tomatoes with juice and wine until blended. (The dish can be made ahead to this point; see Note.) Bake, covered, until meat is tender, about 1½ hours.

Add parsley to rice and mix well. To serve, place rice on a platter and spoon beef and sauce over all.

¼ cup all-purpose flour

½ teaspoon salt

Freshly ground pepper to taste

2 pounds round steak, cut into 1-inch cubes

2 tablespoons vegetable oil

1 cup chopped yellow onion

2 garlic cloves, minced

1 teaspoon paprika

2 cans (14½ ounces each) whole tomatoes, with juice, cut up

½ cup dry red wine

¼ cup chopped fresh parsley

1 cup white long-grain rice, cooked according to package directions (3 cups cooked)

NOTE: If making ahead, refrigerate, then bring to room temperature before baking.

EASY FLANK STEAK IN A TOMATO-BEER MARINADE

Serves 4 to 6

This lean flank steak marinated in a simple blend of ketchup, beer, and soy sauce delivers a lot of flavor. It can be broiled or grilled and is delicious served with fresh corn on the cob (page 214).

In a large glass baking dish, combine ketchup, beer, soy sauce, and garlic and mix well. Add steak and turn to coat. Marinate 1½ to 2 hours in refrigerator, turning occasionally. Bring to room temperature before broiling.

Preheat broiler. Remove steak from marinade and discard marinade. Broil steak 4 inches from heat, about 5 minutes on each side for medium-rare. Transfer to a cutting board and let stand for 5 minutes. Cut into 1-inch strips on the diagonal across the grain to serve.

½   cup ketchup
½   cup flat beer
1   tablespoon soy sauce
2   garlic cloves, minced
1   flank steak (1¾ to 2 pounds)

BARBECUED BEEF ROAST IN THE OVEN

Serves 6, with leftovers

Just the aroma of this meat roasting in the oven will pique your appetite. It takes 1½ hours to cook, but it is worth the wait. Bake some potatoes along with the roast for a weekday family supper. Leftover meat makes good sandwiches the next day.

Preheat oven to 350°F. Place beef in a lightly sprayed or oiled roasting pan or Dutch oven. Season with salt and pepper. In a small bowl, combine ketchup, mustard, horseradish, and Worcestershire sauce and mix well. Spread mixture over meat and arrange onion slices on top. Cover and bake until meat is tender, about 1½ hours.

1   beef top round roast, 1½ inches thick (about 3 pounds)
    Salt and freshly ground pepper to taste
½   cup ketchup
1   tablespoon prepared mustard
1   teaspoon prepared horseradish
1   teaspoon Worcestershire sauce
1   small yellow onion, sliced

NOTE: If desired, to make gravy, blend ¼ cup flour with ½ cup water and stir into pan juices over medium heat until thickened.

SUPPER STEW

Serves 6

Here is a homey, robust main course to serve on a chilly winter night. It requires no browning; just toss all the ingredients together and in an hour and a half you have one big pot of delicious stew for a complete entrée.

Preheat oven to 350°F. In a Dutch oven, combine soy sauce, Worcestershire sauce, flour, salt, and pepper and mix well. Toss beef in soy sauce mixture to coat. Stir in remaining ingredients.

Cover and bake until meat is very tender, about 1½ hours.

NOTE: This is also a good dish to make in a crock pot. Start on high for 15 minutes, then reduce setting to low and cook for 6 to 8 hours.

¼	cup soy sauce
1	teaspoon Worcestershire sauce
¼	cup all-purpose flour
½	teaspoon salt
	Freshly ground pepper to taste
2½	pounds cubed beef stew meat
2	cups baby carrots
4	medium unpeeled new potatoes (about 1½ pounds), scrubbed and halved
1	yellow onion, sliced
2	celery stalks, cut on the diagonal into 1-inch pieces
3	garlic cloves, minced
¼	teaspoon dried thyme
¼	teaspoon dried marjoram
1	cup dry red wine
1½	cups beef broth

BIG BEEF-BEAN STEW

Serves 8

Offer this hearty dish of meat, vegetables, and beans when you want to feed a crowd for supper. Serve with the Romaine, Arugula, and Avocado Salad with Creamy Garlic-Herb Buttermilk Dressing (page 53).

On a piece of waxed paper, mix together flour and 1/4 teaspoon salt. Add beef and toss to coat. In a large skillet over medium heat, warm 2 tablespoons oil. Add meat and brown on all sides, 4 to 5 minutes. Transfer to a plate. Add remaining 1 tablespoon oil, onion, bell pepper, and garlic and sauté until tender, about 5 minutes. Return meat to skillet. Add tomatoes with juice, carrots, thyme, remaining 1 teaspoon salt, pepper, and wine. Reduce heat to medium-low and simmer, covered, for about 1 hour. Add zucchini and beans and simmer, covered, until meat and vegetables are tender, about 30 minutes longer. Serve in bowls.

1/4 cup all-purpose flour

1 1/4 teaspoons salt

2 1/2 pounds cubed beef stew meat

3 tablespoons vegetable oil

1 yellow onion, sliced

1/2 green bell pepper, seeded and cut into 1-inch pieces

1 garlic clove, minced

2 cans (14 1/2 ounces each) whole tomatoes, with juice, cut up

3 or 4 carrots, cut into 1-inch pieces

1/2 teaspoon dried thyme

Freshly ground pepper to taste

1 cup dry red wine

2 zucchini, unpeeled, cut into 1-inch pieces

1 can (15 ounces) red kidney beans, drained and rinsed

FOOD-PROCESSOR MEATBALLS IN ITALIAN TOMATO SAUCE

Serves 6

Your family will start raving as soon as they come in the door about the aroma that fills the air from these wonderful meatballs. A food processor speeds up preparation time and the oven does the browning. Serve over your favorite pasta with Tossed Green Salad with Italian Dressing (page 50).

To make the meatballs, preheat oven to 400°F. Place bread in food processor and process until crumbs form. Transfer crumbs to a large bowl. Add onion and garlic to food processor and process until finely chopped. Add remaining meatball ingredients and pulse to blend. Transfer to the bowl holding the crumbs and mix well with your hands. Form into 1¼-inch meatballs (about 20) and place on a baking sheet. Bake until browned, about 15 minutes.

Meanwhile, make the sauce: In a large saucepan over medium heat, warm olive oil. Add onion and garlic and sauté until tender, about 5 minutes. Add tomatoes with juice, tomato sauce, basil, oregano, salt, and pepper. Reduce heat to low and simmer, uncovered, until flavors are blended, about 15 minutes.

Add browned meatballs to sauce and simmer, uncovered, 10 minutes longer. Sprinkle with Parmesan and serve.

MEATBALLS

1 slice whole-wheat bread, torn up
1 thick yellow onion slice, coarsely chopped
1 garlic clove, coarsely chopped
2 or 3 fresh parsley sprigs
1 pound ground beef or ground turkey
½ pound pork sausage
½ cup whole milk
1 large egg
¼ teaspoon dried oregano
¼ teaspoon dried basil
½ teaspoon salt
   Freshly ground pepper to taste

ITALIAN TOMATO SAUCE

1 tablespoon olive oil
¼ cup chopped yellow onion
1 garlic clove, minced
1 can (16 ounces) plum (Roma) tomatoes, with juice, cut up
1 can (8 ounces) tomato sauce
¼ teaspoon dried basil
¼ teaspoon dried oregano
½ teaspoon salt
   Freshly ground pepper to taste

2 tablespoons freshly grated Parmesan cheese

TORTILLA PIE

Serves 4 to 6

This thrifty, nutritious, and lively supper dish will be a hit with the family. It is so easy, even the kids can make it, with a minimum of supervision. Substitute ground turkey or chicken for the beef, if desired.

Preheat oven to 350°F. In a large skillet over medium heat, combine meat, onion, and garlic and sauté, breaking up meat with a spoon, until meat is browned and onions are tender, 6 to 7 minutes, adding a little oil if needed. Add chiles, tomato sauce, salt, and pepper. Mix well and simmer a few minutes. In a lightly sprayed or oiled 8-by-3-inch deep-dish pie plate, layer 4 tortilla halves, half of the meat-tomato sauce, and half of the cheese. Repeat the layers. Cover the pie plate with aluminum foil and bake until bubbling, about 25 minutes. Let stand for 10 minutes before serving. Cut into 6 wedges and garnish with olives. Pass sour cream in a bowl.

1	pound ground beef
1	cup chopped yellow onion
1	garlic clove, minced
	Vegetable oil, as needed
1	can (4 ounces) diced green chiles, drained
1	can (8 ounces) tomato sauce
½	teaspoon salt
	Freshly ground pepper to taste
4	corn tortillas, halved
2	cups grated pepper Jack cheese
1	cup pitted black olives
	Sour cream for serving

HAMBURGER STROGANOFF

Serves 4

You won't have any trouble rounding up the family for this popular supper. Serve with Poppy Seed Noodles (page 193) or Smashed Potatoes with Blue Cheese and Chives (page 217).

In a large skillet over medium heat, combine beef and onion and sauté until beef is browned and onions are tender, about 5 minutes, adding a little oil if needed. Add broth, water, ketchup, Worcestershire sauce, salt, and pepper. Simmer, uncovered, until flavors are blended, about 10 minutes, stirring occasionally. Remove from heat and stir in sour cream. Reheat over low heat for a few minutes and serve immediately.

1   pound ground beef
½   cup chopped yellow onion
     Vegetable oil, as needed
1   can (10½ ounces) beef broth
½   cup water
1   tablespoon ketchup
1   teaspoon Worcestershire sauce
¼   teaspoon salt
     Freshly ground pepper to taste
½   cup sour cream

OVEN PORK CHOPS WITH BARBECUE SAUCE

Serves 4

These chops are browned on top of the stove, then baked in the oven in a zesty barbecue sauce. Serve with Poppy Seed Noodles (page 193) for an easy, casual supper.

Preheat oven to 350°F. In a large skillet over medium-high heat, warm 1 tablespoon oil. Add pork chops and brown, 6 to 7 minutes on each side. Season with salt and pepper. Transfer chops to a lightly sprayed or oiled 2-quart casserole and set aside.

Reduce heat under skillet to medium and sauté onion until tender, about 5 minutes. Add more oil if needed. Add remaining ingredients and simmer a few minutes. Pour over the chops in the casserole. Cover and bake until chops are tender and barely pink in the center, 25 to 30 minutes.

1	to 2 tablespoons vegetable oil
4	bone-in pork chops (about 1¾ pounds)
	Salt and freshly ground pepper to taste
½	cup chopped yellow onion
1	can (8 ounces) tomato sauce
¼	cup ketchup
1	tablespoon brown sugar
1	tablespoon cider vinegar
2	teaspoons Worcestershire sauce
2	to 3 drops Tabasco sauce

PORK CHOPS WITH ORANGE GLAZE
Serves 4

For a busy weeknight supper, a simple topping of orange marmalade and Dijon mustard enlivens the flavor of these chops. Bake sweet potatoes along with the chops.

Preheat oven to 350°F. In a medium sauce-pan over medium-high heat, warm oil. Add pork chops and brown, 6 to 7 minutes on each side. Season with salt and pepper. Transfer chops to a lightly sprayed or oiled 8-by-10-inch glass baking dish.

In a small bowl, mix together marmalade and mustard. Spread evenly over the chops. Cover and bake until chops are tender and barely pink in the center, 25 to 30 minutes.

2   teaspoons vegetable oil

4   bone-in pork chops (about 1¾ pounds)
    Salt and freshly ground pepper to taste

3   tablespoons orange marmalade

1   teaspoon Dijon mustard

PORK CHOPS WITH SOUR CREAM-DILL SAUCE

Serves 4

This outstanding recipe of pork chops simmered in a delicious sour cream–dill sauce will become a favorite supper dish. Serve with noodles to absorb some of the flavorful sauce.

In a large skillet over medium-high heat, warm 1 tablespoon olive oil. Add pork chops and brown, 6 to 7 minutes on each side. Season with salt and pepper. Transfer chops to a plate. Reduce heat under skillet to medium and add remaining 1 tablespoon olive oil, bell pepper, and onion and sauté until vegetables are tender, about 5 minutes. Add broth and simmer about 2 minutes.

In a small bowl, mix together sour cream, flour, mustard, paprika, and dill. Remove pan from heat and stir in sour cream mixture. Return chops to the skillet. Reduce heat to low and simmer, turning once, until chops are barely pink on the inside, about 12 minutes. Serve chops with sauce spooned over and garnish with green onions.

2	tablespoons olive oil
4	bone-in pork chops (about 1¾ pounds)
	Salt and freshly ground pepper to taste
½	red bell pepper, seeded and sliced into ½-inch strips
½	cup chopped yellow onion
1	cup chicken broth
1	cup sour cream
1	tablespoon all-purpose flour
2	tablespoons Dijon mustard
1	teaspoon paprika
2	tablespoons chopped fresh dill or 1 teaspoon dried dill
3	green onions, including some tender green tops, sliced

SALSA PORK CHOPS

Serves 4

If you are coming home late from work, this recipe is a quick, easy supper option. Serve on a bed of rice along with the Orange, Cucumber, and Red Onion Salad with Lime-Cumin Dressing (page 54).

In a large skillet over medium-high heat, warm oil. Add pork chops and brown, 6 to 7 minutes on each side. Season with salt and pepper. Transfer chops to a plate. In the same skillet, combine salsa and pineapple with juice. Bring to a boil. Return chops to the skillet, reduce heat to medium-low, and simmer, covered, 10 minutes, turning once. Remove lid, turn chops, and cook until barely pink in the center, about 2 minutes longer.

Mound rice on a warmed platter. Arrange chops and sauce on top and garnish with cilantro sprigs.

2   teaspoons vegetable oil

4   boneless pork chops (about 1½ pounds)
    Salt and freshly ground pepper to taste

1   cup Fresh Tomato Salsa (page 71) or good-quality purchased salsa

1   can (8 ounces) crushed pineapple, with juice

1   cup long-grain white rice, cooked according to package directions (3 cups cooked)
    Fresh cilantro or parsley sprigs for garnish

HARVEST PORK ROAST

Serves 6

Center an autumn supper around this tender, juicy roast and some seasonal vegetables. The easy topping of spicy applesauce and Dijon mustard keeps the roast moist and adds flavor while it bakes. Serve with Zucchini Bake (page 225) and Apple-Berry Crisp (page 312) for dessert.

In a medium bowl, mix together applesauce, mustard, salt, and pepper. Place pork in a large roasting pan with a rack. Spread applesauce mixture on top, covering the roast completely. Let stand 1 hour at room temperature.

Preheat oven to 350°F. Bake, uncovered, until meat is browned and slightly pink on the inside or until an instant-read thermometer registers 150° to 155°F, about 1 hour and 45 minutes. Transfer to a platter and let stand for 10 minutes before carving.

1 cup spicy applesauce
1 tablespoon Dijon mustard
½ teaspoon salt
   Freshly ground pepper to taste
1 boneless pork roast (about 3 pounds)

ITALIAN SAUSAGE, PEPPERS, AND MUSHROOMS

Serves 4

Serve this colorful skillet dish of sausage, bell peppers, and mushrooms over rice or pasta. Easy Brownies (page 326) and ice cream make a good dessert.

In a saucepan over high heat, combine sausage with water to cover. Bring to a boil, reduce heat to medium-low, and cook, uncovered, 10 minutes. Drain sausage and cut into ½ inch slices.

In a large skillet over medium heat, warm oil. Add bell peppers, garlic, and mushrooms and sauté until vegetables are tender, about 5 minutes. Return sausage to the skillet and mix well. Add tomatoes with juice and seasonings and simmer, uncovered, until flavors are blended, about 15 minutes, stirring occasionally. Serve, sprinkled with parsley.

½	pound Italian sausage links
1	tablespoon vegetable oil
½	green bell pepper, seeded and cut into large bite-sized pieces
½	red bell pepper, seeded and cut into large bite-sized pieces
2	garlic cloves, minced
4	ounces mushrooms, sliced
1	can (14½ ounces) whole tomatoes, with juice, cut up
¼	teaspoon dried oregano
¼	teaspoon dried basil
	Salt and freshly ground pepper to taste
¼	cup chopped fresh parsley

KIELBASA AND SAUERKRAUT

Serves 6

Kielbasa and sauerkraut are simmered in beer in this hearty supper dish. Kielbasa is fully cooked smoked sausage that comes in large links, but other sausage may be used. Serve with rye bread and cold beer or apple cider.

In a Dutch oven or large skillet over medium heat, melt butter. Add onion and garlic and sauté until tender, about 5 minutes. Add sauerkraut, beer, sausage, and caraway seed and mix well. Reduce heat to medium-low and simmer, uncovered, stirring occasionally, until flavors are blended and liquid is almost gone, about 30 minutes.

1	tablespoon butter
½	cup chopped yellow onion
1	garlic clove, minced
1	jar (16 ounces) sauerkraut, drained
1	bottle (12 ounces) flat beer
1	pound kielbasa sausage, cut into ¾-inch slices
1	teaspoon caraway or fennel seed

SAUSAGE LOAF

Serves 4

Bake Twice-Baked Potatoes (page 219) along with this sausage loaf for a classic combination. Any leftover loaf makes delicious sandwiches the next day.

Preheat oven to 350°F. In a large bowl, whisk together egg and milk. Add sausage, crackers, onion, and pepper and mix well with your hands. Place in a lightly sprayed or oiled 4-by-8-by-2½-inch loaf pan and bake until sausage is no longer pink, about 1 hour. Pour off excess grease, if necessary. Let stand for 5 minutes. Remove from pan and slice.

1   large egg
¼   cup whole milk
1   pound bulk pork sausage
¾   cup crushed saltines (about 15)
¼   cup finely chopped yellow onion
       Freshly ground pepper to taste

NOTE: If you are using a mild sausage, you can add more seasoning to taste.

HAM AND POTATO CASSEROLE

Serves 4 to 6

Ham and potatoes complement each other in this substantial supper dish. Serve with asparagus. Use the slicing blade on a food processor to make quick work of the potatoes.

Preheat oven to 350°F. In a lightly sprayed or oiled 8-by-10-inch glass baking dish, layer half of the potatoes. Sprinkle with flour and salt and pepper to taste. Layer on all of the ham, half of the onion slices, and half of the cheese. Add remaining potatoes and season again with salt and pepper. Add remaining onions and top with remaining cheese. Pour milk over all, cover with aluminum foil, and bake until bubbly and potatoes are tender, about 1 hour. Remove foil and let stand for 5 minutes before serving.

4   medium russet potatoes (about 2 pounds), peeled and sliced
1   tablespoon all-purpose flour
    Salt and freshly ground pepper to taste
1   pound cubed cooked ham
1   small white onion, sliced
2   cups grated Cheddar cheese
¾   cup whole milk

SKILLET LAMB CHOPS IN ORANGE SAUCE

Serves 4

For a last-minute supper, try these fast and easy orange-flavored lamb chops. Serve with plain rice or Oven Brown Rice and Vegetables (page 194).

In a large skillet over medium-high heat, warm oil. Add lamb chops, season with salt and pepper, and brown, about 3 minutes on each side.

In a small bowl, whisk together orange juice, brown sugar, vinegar, zest, and rosemary. Pour off excess fat in the skillet and pour the orange juice mixture over the chops. Reduce heat to medium-low, cover, and cook until chops are tender and slightly pink in the center, about 10 minutes, turning once. Transfer chops to a serving platter and spoon some pan juices over. Garnish with orange segments.

1½ tablespoons vegetable oil

8 lamb chops, about 1 inch thick (about 6 ounces each)

Salt and freshly ground pepper to taste

¾ cup orange juice

2 tablespoons firmly packed brown sugar

1 tablespoon white wine vinegar

1 teaspoon grated orange zest

1 teaspoon dried rosemary

Orange segments for garnish

LAMB CHOPS WITH CRUMB TOPPING

Serves 4

A coating of seasoned bread crumbs adds a crunchy topping to these broiled lamb chops. Serve with Spinach Salad with Cucumber, Mushrooms, and Feta Cheese with Lemon-Dijon Vinaigrette (page 47).

Preheat broiler. In a small bowl, stir together bread crumbs, rosemary, parsley, mustard, and 1 tablespoon olive oil and set aside. In another small bowl, combine garlic, salt and pepper, and remaining 1 tablespoon olive oil. Brush lamb chops on both sides with garlic oil. Place chops on an aluminum foil–lined broiler pan and broil 4 minutes on each side. Spread bread-crumb mixture evenly on top of each chop. Broil until topping is bubbly, 1 to 2 minutes longer. Transfer to warmed plates and garnish with rosemary sprigs. Serve immediately.

½ cup coarse dried bread crumbs

1 tablespoon chopped fresh rosemary or 1 teaspoon dried rosemary, plus fresh rosemary sprigs for garnish

2 tablespoons finely chopped fresh parsley

1 teaspoon Dijon mustard

2 tablespoons olive oil

1 garlic clove, minced

¼ teaspoon salt

Freshly ground pepper to taste

8 lamb chops, 1 inch thick (about 6 ounces each)

LAMB AND TURKEY LOAF

Serves 6 to 8

This lean and healthful loaf was developed by my son, Scott, who loves meatloaf but does not eat beef. It makes a large loaf to serve hot as a main dish and cold in delicious sandwiches the next day. The Cranberry-Horseradish Relish adds some extra zing to this loaf.

Preheat oven to 350°F. Place oats in food processor and process until finely chopped. Add turkey, tomato, celery, egg, soy sauce, and Worcestershire sauce and process until blended. Transfer to a medium bowl. Place lamb in the food processor and process briefly. Add to the bowl holding the other ingredients and mix well with your hands. Place in a lightly sprayed or oiled 8-by-8-inch glass baking dish. Bake until firm, about 1 hour. Let stand for 5 minutes. Serve with Cranberry-Horseradish Relish.

1   cup quick-cooking rolled oats

1   pound ground turkey

1   plum (Roma) tomato, cut up

1   celery stalk, cut up

1   large egg

2   to 3 tablespoons soy sauce

½   teaspoon Worcestershire sauce

1   pound ground lamb
    Cranberry-Horseradish Relish (recipe follows)

CRANBERRY-HORSERADISH RELISH

The horseradish adds a surprising zippy flavor to this raw cranberry relish. This is also good on other fish, poultry, and ham.

Place all ingredients in a food processor and pulse until coarsely chopped. Let stand at room temperature before serving. Cover and store leftover relish in the refrigerator for up to 2 days.

Makes about 2½ cups

1   package (12 ounces) fresh uncooked cranberries (about 3 cups), rinsed

3   tablespoons walnut pieces

¾   cup sugar

2   to 3 teaspoons prepared horseradish

2   tablespoons fresh orange juice

CHICKEN

CHAPTER 6

CLASSIC AND CONTEMPORARY CHICKEN SUPPER RECIPES

Chicken is one of the most popular entrées served for supper. It is healthful, inexpensive, versatile, readily available, and appeals to all ages. It is an excellent source of protein and is low in calories when the skin is removed. Chicken can be baked, broiled, grilled, sautéed, or used as the foundation for casseroles and stews. The mild flavor lends itself well to a variety of seasonings and sauces, and is easily adapted to many ethnic dishes.

Chicken can be purchased whole, cut up, or in specialty packs of choice pieces (breasts, thighs, and drumsticks), fresh or frozen. Store all chicken, lightly covered, in the refrigerator until ready to use. Thaw frozen chicken overnight in the refrigerator, not at room temperature. Rinse chicken under cold water before cooking and dry with paper towels. Trim off excess skin and fat with kitchen shears. To remove skin, if desired, hold the skin with a paper towel and pull it off. Wash your work surfaces, hands, and utensils with soapy water after working with chicken (or any raw meat). Chicken must be fully cooked, with no pink showing in the center when cut with a sharp knife.

You will find a large selection of chicken recipes in this chapter suitable for supper, including Herbed Parmesan Chicken (page 114), Chicken Dijon (page 117), Baked Mustard-Coated Chicken Breasts (page 121), Lemon Roasted Whole Chicken with Garlic and New Potatoes (page 130), and Spicy Chicken Tamale Pie (page 131).

HERBED PARMESAN CHICKEN

Serves 4

This is one of those recipes that are easy to prepare, go together fast, and will suit everyone in the family. Serve with Twice-Baked Potatoes (page 219) and Steamed Herbed Carrots and Broccoli (page 208).

Preheat oven to 350°F. Pour buttermilk into a pie plate. On a large piece of waxed paper, mix together bread crumbs, Parmesan, garlic powder, basil, thyme, oregano, salt, and pepper. Dip chicken pieces in buttermilk and then roll in crumb mixture to coat evenly. Arrange chicken in a lightly sprayed or oiled 9-by-13-inch glass baking dish. Bake, uncovered, until chicken is lightly browned and is no longer pink in the center, about 1 hour.

½ cup buttermilk

1¼ cups coarse dried sourdough bread crumbs

⅓ cup freshly grated Parmesan cheese

¼ teaspoon garlic powder

½ teaspoon dried basil

¼ teaspoon dried thyme

¼ teaspoon dried oregano

½ teaspoon salt

Freshly ground pepper to taste

1 chicken (3 to 3½ pounds), cut into serving pieces, excess fat and skin trimmed

CURRIED CHICKEN

Serves 6

As this chicken, dipped in a pungent sauce, bakes in the oven, it produces a wonderful aroma and develops a distinctive flavor. Serve with rice, and pass additional soy sauce.

Preheat oven to 350°F. In a medium bowl, whisk together honey, mustard, curry powder, and soy sauce. Dip chicken in mixture and place in a lightly sprayed or oiled 9-by-13-inch glass baking dish. Bake, uncovered, 30 minutes. Turn and continue to bake until chicken is no longer pink in the center, about 30 minutes longer.

¼ cup honey

2 teaspoons mustard

¼ teaspoon curry powder

½ cup soy sauce

1 chicken (3½ to 4 pounds), cut into serving pieces, excess fat and skin trimmed

CRISPY BAKED CHICKEN

Serves 4

A buttermilk-cornmeal mixture adds a tangy flavor and crunchy coating to this chicken. For a contrasting vegetable, serve Broccoli with Herb Butter (page 204).

Preheat oven to 400°F. In a shallow dish, whisk together buttermilk and mustard. On a large piece of waxed paper, mix cornmeal, flour, salt, and pepper. Dip chicken in buttermilk mixture, then in the flour mixture to coat evenly. Melt butter in a 9-by-13-inch glass baking dish in the oven. Place chicken in the dish and turn to coat. Bake, uncovered, 30 minutes. Turn and continue to bake until chicken is no longer pink in the center, about 30 minutes longer.

½   cup buttermilk

2   tablespoons Dijon mustard

½   cup cornmeal

½   cup all-purpose flour

1   teaspoon salt

¼   teaspoon freshly ground pepper

1   chicken (3½ to 4 pounds), cut into serving pieces, excess fat and skin trimmed

¼   cup (½ stick) butter

CHICKEN DIJON

Serves 4

Choice chicken pieces are baked in the oven and then topped with an elegant Dijon Cheese Sauce for this easy company supper. Serve with Mixed Greens, Avocado, and Mushroom Salad with Tangy Red Dressing (page 51).

Preheat oven to 350°F. In a 9-by-13-inch glass baking dish, melt butter with oil in the oven. Add chicken and turn to coat. Season with salt and pepper. Bake 30 minutes. Turn chicken over and pour cheese sauce over. Bake, uncovered, until bubbly, about 30 minutes longer.

1	tablespoon butter
1	tablespoon vegetable oil
1	chicken (3½ to 4 pounds), cut into serving pieces (use drumsticks, thighs, and breasts), excess fat and skin trimmed
	Salt and freshly ground pepper to taste
	Dijon Cheese Sauce (recipe follows)

DIJON CHEESE SAUCE

In a medium saucepan over medium heat, melt butter. Add flour and stir until bubbly. Add broth and stir until thickened, about 2 minutes. Reduce heat to low and stir in wine, cheese, mustard, tarragon, salt, and parsley. Simmer until cheese melts and flavors are blended.

Makes about 1½ cups

2	tablespoons butter
2	tablespoons all-purpose flour
1	cup chicken broth
3	tablespoons dry white wine
¼	cup grated Cheddar cheese
1	tablespoon Dijon mustard
½	teaspoon dried tarragon
¼	teaspoon salt
3	tablespoons chopped fresh parsley

CHICKEN WITH CREAMY MUSTARD-TARRAGON SAUCE

Serves 4

Deglazing the pan with wine after sautéing the chicken creates an intense sauce for this rich, elegant dish. Serve with a fresh fruit plate and Butterscotch-Chocolate Chip Bars (page 325) for a special supper.

Place chicken breasts between 2 pieces of plastic wrap and pound to about ⅜ inch thick. Cut into bite-sized pieces. On a large piece of waxed paper, mix flour, ¼ teaspoon salt, and pepper. Add chicken and turn to coat.

In a large skillet over medium heat, melt butter. Add chicken and brown, about 5 minutes on each side. Transfer to a plate. Add wine and broth to skillet. Raise temperature to high and boil until liquid is reduced by half, about 2 minutes. Reduce heat to medium and whisk in half-and-half, mustard, tarragon, parsley, and remaining ¼ teaspoon salt until blended. Return chicken to pan and reheat for several minutes. Serve chicken with sauce.

4	large boned and skinned chicken breast halves (about 8 ounces each)
¼	cup all-purpose flour
½	teaspoon salt
	Freshly ground pepper to taste
2	tablespoons butter
½	cup dry white wine
½	cup chicken broth
½	cup half-and-half or whole milk
2	teaspoons Dijon mustard
1	teaspoon dried tarragon
1	tablespoon chopped fresh parsley

CHICKEN AND CHEESE

Serves 4

Simplicity is the key to this chicken recipe. Chicken breasts are topped with mushrooms and cheese and then baked in the oven. Twice-Baked Potatoes (page 219) can be baked at the same time for an easy supper.

Preheat oven to 350°F. Place chicken in a lightly sprayed or oiled 8-by-8-inch glass baking dish. Brush with oil and sprinkle with oregano and season with salt and pepper. Divide mushrooms and parsley evenly among tops of breasts. Cover each with a cheese slice. Bake, uncovered, until chicken is no longer pink in the center and cheese is melted, 35 to 40 minutes.

4   large boned and skinned chicken breast halves (about 8 ounces each)
    Vegetable oil for brushing
¼   teaspoon dried oregano
    Salt and freshly ground pepper to taste
4   ounces mushrooms, sliced
3   tablespoons chopped fresh parsley
4   slices Monterey Jack cheese

CHICKEN BREASTS, SOUTHWESTERN STYLE

Serves 4 to 6

These baked, crunchy coated chicken breasts topped with a dollop of sour cream, salsa, and avocado slices when served on a platter make a colorful presentation. Serve with Double Corn Polenta (page 199).

Preheat oven to 400°F. In a large shallow bowl, whisk together lime juice, honey, oil, salt, and pepper. Add chicken and turn to coat and let stand 10 minutes. Spread crushed chips on a large piece of waxed paper. Remove chicken from lime juice mixture, reserving leftover juice, and roll in chips to coat evenly. Place in a lightly sprayed or oiled 8-by-10-inch glass baking dish. Pour remaining juice over all. Bake until chicken is no longer pink in the center and coating is crisp, about 35 minutes. Transfer to a warm platter. Top each breast with a dollop each of salsa and sour cream and a few avocado slices. Garnish with lime wedges.

Juice of 1 lime

2 tablespoons honey

1 tablespoon vegetable oil

¼ teaspoon salt

Freshly ground pepper to taste

6 large boned and skinned chicken breast halves (about 8 ounces each)

1 cup finely crushed corn chips or tortilla chips

½ cup Fresh Tomato Salsa (page 71) or good-quality purchased tomato salsa

¼ cup sour cream

1 avocado, peeled, pitted, and sliced

Lime wedges for garnish

BAKED MUSTARD-COATED CHICKEN BREASTS

Serves 4 to 6

These mustardy chicken breasts make an easy oven supper served with baked sweet potatoes and Spinach with Bacon and Egg Topping (page 222).

Preheat oven to 400°F. In a large shallow bowl, whisk together mustard, olive oil, vinegar, rosemary, salt, and white pepper. Place bread crumbs on a large piece of waxed paper. Dip chicken in mustard mixture, then roll in crumbs to coat evenly. Place in a lightly sprayed or oiled 8-by-10-inch glass baking dish. Bake, uncovered, until chicken is no longer pink in the center and coating is golden brown, about 35 minutes.

3	tablespoons Dijon mustard
1	tablespoon olive oil
1	tablespoon white wine vinegar
½	teaspoon dried rosemary
¼	teaspoon salt
⅛	teaspoon white pepper
¾	cup fine dried bread crumbs
6	large boned and skinned chicken breast halves (about 8 ounces each)

SMOKY CHICKEN BREASTS

Serves 4 to 6

Wrapping chicken breasts in bacon imparts a salty, smoky flavor and keeps them moist as they bake. Serve with Steamed Baby Carrots (page 211).

Preheat oven to 375°F. Sprinkle each chicken breast generously with salt and pepper, wrap each with a bacon strip, and secure bacon with a toothpick. Place in a lightly sprayed or oiled 8-by-10-inch glass baking dish.

In a small bowl, mix together melted butter, Worcestershire sauce, and lemon juice and pour over chicken. Bake until bacon is crisp and chicken is no longer pink in the center, about 35 minutes.

6   large boned and skinned chicken breast halves (about 8 ounces each)
     Salt and freshly ground pepper
6   slices lean bacon
¼   cup (½ stick) butter, melted
1   tablespoon Worcestershire sauce
1   tablespoon fresh lemon juice

TANGY-SAUCED BAKED CHICKEN BREASTS

Serves 4 to 6

Prepare this dish at least 4 hours ahead to allow the flavors to develop. Make it in the morning and pop it in the oven after a busy day; enjoy a glass of wine while it bakes. Add Broccoli with Herb Butter (page 204) to the menu.

In a large bowl, whisk together yogurt, sour cream, mustard, garlic, lemon juice, Worcestershire sauce, paprika, salt, and pepper. Add chicken and turn to coat. Cover and marinate in the refrigerator several hours. Bring chicken to room temperature before baking.

Preheat oven to 350°F. Place bread crumbs on a large piece of waxed paper. Remove chicken from marinade and roll in bread crumbs to coat evenly. Place in a lightly sprayed or oiled 8-by-10-inch glass baking dish. Bake, uncovered, until chicken is no longer pink in the center, about 35 minutes.

½ cup plain nonfat yogurt

½ cup sour cream

1 tablespoon Dijon mustard

1 garlic clove, minced

2 tablespoons fresh lemon juice

1 teaspoon Worcestershire sauce

½ teaspoon paprika

½ teaspoon salt

Freshly ground pepper to taste

6 large boned and skinned chicken breast halves (about 8 ounces each)

½ cup fine dried bread crumbs

CHICKEN THIGHS WITH ORANGE-SOY SAUCE

Serves 4

Offer these flavorful chicken thighs baked in an orange-soy sauce spooned over fluffy rice. Serve with avocado and orange slices.

Preheat oven to 350°F. In a medium skillet over medium-high heat, warm oil. Add chicken thighs and brown, 6 or 7 minutes on each side. Transfer to a lightly sprayed or oiled 8-by-8-inch glass baking dish. In a bowl or cup, whisk together orange juice, soy sauce, zest, honey, salt, and ginger and pour over chicken. Bake, uncovered, 30 minutes. Baste with sauce. Turn and sprinkle with sesame seeds. Bake until chicken is no longer pink in the center and seeds are toasted, about 15 minutes longer.

1	tablespoon vegetable oil
6	boned and skinned chicken thighs (1½ to 2 pounds)
¼	cup orange juice
¼	cup soy sauce
1	teaspoon grated orange zest
1	tablespoon honey
¼	teaspoon salt
¼	teaspoon ground ginger
1	tablespoon sesame seeds

MEDITERRANEAN CHICKEN THIGHS WITH OLIVES

Serves 4 to 6

This chicken dish with tomatoes and olives makes an impressive, impromptu company supper. Orzo is a good accompaniment. When I started to prepare this dish, I thought it had too many steps to include in this book of easy recipes, but after serving it to guests who raved about it, I decided it was too good to leave out. I hope you like it, too.

On a large piece of waxed paper, mix flour, paprika, oregano, thyme, salt, and pepper. Roll chicken in mixture to coat evenly. (Alternatively, place mixture in a paper bag, add chicken pieces, and shake well.) Reserve remaining flour.

In a Dutch oven over medium-high heat, warm 1½ tablespoons olive oil. Add chicken and brown on all sides, about 15 minutes. Transfer to a plate. Add remaining ½ tablespoon oil, onion, garlic, and bell pepper to pot and sauté until vegetables are tender, about 5 minutes. Add tomatoes with juice and wine. Add remaining flour and stir until slightly thickened, about 2 minutes.

Preheat oven to 350°F. Return chicken to the pot. Cover and bake 45 minutes. Add olives and bake until chicken is no longer pink in the center, about 15 minutes longer. Serve with orzo, spooning vegetables and sauce over.

¼	cup all-purpose flour
1	teaspoon paprika
½	teaspoon dried oregano
½	teaspoon dried thyme
½	teaspoon salt
	Freshly ground pepper to taste
4	chicken thighs (1½ to 2 pounds)
4	drumsticks (1½ to 2 pounds)
2	tablespoons olive oil
½	yellow onion, sliced
2	garlic cloves, minced
½	cup chopped red bell pepper
1	can (14½ ounces) whole tomatoes with juice, cut up
2	tablespoons dry white wine
¼	cup pimiento-stuffed green olives
½	cup pitted Kalamata olives or other black olives
1	cup orzo, cooked according to package directions and drained

HERBED CHICKEN THIGHS IN TOMATO SAUCE

Serves 4

Chicken thighs are flavorful and moist and appeal to those who prefer dark chicken meat over white. Here the thighs are seasoned and baked in a tomato sauce. For a side dish, try Italian Sautéed Peppers (page 216).

Preheat oven to 350°F. Place chicken in a lightly sprayed or oiled 8-by-8-inch glass baking dish. Sprinkle with salt and pepper, thyme, basil, oregano, and parsley. Arrange onion slices on top. Pour tomato sauce over all and sprinkle with Parmesan. Bake, uncovered, until chicken is no longer pink in the center, about 45 minutes.

6	boned and skinned chicken thighs (1½ to 2 pounds)
	Salt and freshly ground pepper to taste
¼	teaspoon dried thyme
¼	teaspoon dried basil
¼	teaspoon dried oregano
¼	cup chopped fresh parsley
4	yellow onion slices, separated
1	can (8 ounces) tomato sauce
¼	cup freshly grated Parmesan cheese

CHICKEN BOBSIE

Serves 4

This is one of the easiest chicken recipes I know, but it is also impressive, because each person gets a full chicken quarter. The quarters are coated with butter, then generously sprinkled with paprika, salt, and pepper and baked until tender and golden brown. Serve with Parmesan-Pecan Rice (page 195).

Preheat oven to 350°F. Place chicken in a lightly sprayed or oiled 9-by-13-inch glass baking dish. Pour melted butter over. Sprinkle generously with paprika to cover. Season with salt and pepper. Bake, uncovered, basting with juices once or twice, until skin is golden and chicken is no longer pink in the center, about 1 hour.

1 chicken (3 to 3½ pounds), quartered, excess skin and fat trimmed

¼ cup (½ stick) butter, melted

Paprika for sprinkling on top

Salt and freshly ground pepper to taste

BAKED ORANGE-ROSEMARY CHICKEN

Serves 4

Here chicken quarters are seasoned with a flavorful marinade of orange juice and rosemary, then baked in the oven. Onion Rice (page 197) goes well with this dish.

In a medium bowl, whisk together all marinade ingredients. Place chicken in a lightly sprayed or oiled 9-by-13-inch glass baking dish. Pour marinade over. Cover and refrigerate several hours, turning once. Bring chicken to room temperature before baking.

Preheat oven to 350°F. Bake chicken in the marinade, skin side up, basting with juices once or twice, until it is no longer pink in the center, about 1 hour. Garnish with orange segments.

ORANGE MARINADE

2 tablespoons vegetable oil

½ cup orange juice

1 tablespoon honey

1 tablespoon Dijon mustard

1 teaspoon Worcestershire sauce

2 garlic cloves, minced

1 teaspoon grated orange zest

1 tablespoon snipped fresh rosemary or 1 teaspoon dried rosemary

½ teaspoon salt

Dash of white pepper

1 whole chicken (3½ to 4 pounds), quartered, excess skin and fat trimmed

Orange segments for garnish

BAKED CHICKEN AND RICE WITH HONEY-MUSTARD SAUCE

Serves 4

This dish appeals to busy people because browning the chicken is not necessary. The honey-mustard sauce rounds out the flavors of this complete entrée.

Preheat oven to 350°F. Spread rice in a lightly sprayed or oiled 9-by-13-inch glass baking dish. Arrange chicken on top and pour broth over. Cover tightly with aluminum foil and bake for 45 minutes.

In a medium bowl, whisk together yogurt, honey, mustard, soy sauce, ginger, salt, and pepper. Uncover baking dish and spread yogurt mixture on chicken. Bake, uncovered, until rice is tender and chicken is no longer pink in the center, about 15 minutes longer.

1 cup long-grain white rice

1 chicken (3½ to 4 pounds), cut into serving pieces, excess skin and fat trimmed

2¼ cups hot chicken broth

½ cup plain nonfat yogurt

¼ cup honey

2 tablespoons Dijon mustard

1 tablespoon soy sauce

½ teaspoon ground ginger

¼ teaspoon salt

Freshly ground pepper to taste

LEMON-ROASTED WHOLE CHICKEN WITH GARLIC AND NEW POTATOES

Serves 4 to 6

Lemon juice, tarragon, and garlic flavor this chicken as it bakes with potatoes for an easy oven supper. Romaine, Arugula, and Avocado Salad with Creamy Garlic-Herb Buttermilk Dressing (page 53) makes a nice accompaniment.

Preheat oven to 350°F. Place chicken in a lightly sprayed or oiled roasting pan and brush with oil. Sprinkle cavity with ¼ teaspoon salt and pepper. Add lemon half to the cavity. Bake, uncovered, 45 minutes.

Add potatoes to the pan. In a small bowl or cup, combine juice from 1 lemon, lemon zest, melted butter, wine, garlic, tarragon, and remaining ¼ teaspoon salt and pour over chicken and potatoes.

Bake, basting several times with juices, until chicken is lightly browned and is no longer pink in the center and potatoes are tender, about 45 minutes longer. Transfer chicken to a platter and let stand for 10 minutes. Remove lemon half and discard. Arrange potatoes around chicken and pour pan juices over all.

1   large chicken (4 to 5 pounds), rinsed and patted dry
    Vegetable oil for brushing
½   teaspoon salt
    Freshly ground pepper to taste
1½ lemons, 1 juiced and ½ for the cavity
4   to 6 garlic cloves, minced
12 small (1½-inch) unpeeled new potatoes (about 1½ pounds), scrubbed
    Grated lemon zest from ½ lemon
3   tablespoons butter, melted
½   cup dry white wine
1   teaspoon dried tarragon

SPICY CHICKEN TAMALE PIE
Serves 8

In this version of a Mexican tamale, the chicken is combined with vegetables and blanketed with a cornmeal topping. Serve with Orange, Cucumber, and Red Onion Salad with Lime-Cumin Dressing (page 54).

TOPPING

1	cup yellow cornmeal
3 1/2	cups water
1/2	teaspoon salt

1	tablespoon vegetable oil
1	cup chopped yellow onion
1/2	cup chopped green bell pepper
1	garlic clove, minced
1	can (14 1/2 ounces) Mexican-recipe stewed tomatoes, with juice (see Note)
1	teaspoon chili powder
1/2	teaspoon dried oregano
1/2	teaspoon salt
	Freshly ground pepper to taste
1	can (15 ounces) kidney beans, drained and rinsed
1	cup corn kernels, fresh or frozen
2	cups cubed cooked chicken (see Note, page 30)
2	cups grated Cheddar cheese

To make the topping, in a medium bowl, mix cornmeal with 1 cup water. In a medium saucepan over high heat, bring remaining 2 1/2 cups water and salt to a boil. Slowly stir cornmeal mixture into the boiling water, stirring occasionally (see Note). Reduce heat to low and simmer, uncovered, stirring constantly, until cornmeal mixture is thick and smooth, about 5 minutes. Remove from heat and set aside.

In a large skillet over medium heat, warm oil. Add onion, bell pepper, and garlic and sauté until vegetables are tender, about 5 minutes. Add tomatoes, seasonings, beans, and corn and simmer, uncovered, to blend flavors, about 10 minutes. Stir in the chicken.

Preheat oven to 350°F. Pour the chicken mixture into a lightly sprayed or oiled 9-by-13-inch glass baking dish. Spread cornmeal mixture evenly over the top and sprinkle with the cheese.

Bake, uncovered, until bubbly, about 30 minutes. Let stand 10 minutes before serving.

NOTES: Use a long-handled spoon to stir the cornmeal. It tends to splash and can cause burns.

Mexican-recipe tomatoes have traditional Mexican seasonings added and are available at most supermarkets.

EGG DISHES

CHAPTER 7

EASY EGG SUPPER DISHES

Eggs are extremely versatile and can be prepared in many ways in a matter of minutes for a satisfying and inexpensive supper.

These recipes call for large eggs. When buying eggs, it is important to check the expiration date and reject any eggs that are cracked. Store eggs in the carton in the refrigerator for up to 1 month, but they have the best quality and flavor if used within a week of purchase.

Eggs are a good source of protein, iron, phosphorous, vitamins A and D, and are now considered a healthy addition to your diet.

Add some of these appetizing recipes to your supper menus. You'll enjoy the Ham and Cheese Omelet (page 137); Egg-Sausage-Chile Bake (page 138); Baked Herbed Zucchini Frittata (page 141); Egg, Ham, and Chile Strata (page 144); and other evening egg creations in this chapter.

SCRAMBLED SUPPER EGGS

Serves 4

Serve these colorful eggs, flecked with tomatoes, basil, and cheese, with toasted English muffins and cantaloupe or watermelon wedges.

In a medium bowl, whisk together eggs, milk, salt, and pepper. Fold in cheese, basil, parsley, and tomato. In a large nonstick skillet over medium heat, melt butter and swirl to coat bottom of the skillet. When butter foams, add egg mixture all at once. Let set for 20 seconds. Stir until light and fluffy and almost dry, about 2 minutes. Sprinkle with Parmesan and serve immediately.

6	large eggs
2	tablespoons whole milk
¼	teaspoon salt
	Freshly ground pepper to taste
1	cup grated mozzarella cheese
1	tablespoon chopped fresh basil or 1 teaspoon dried basil
2	tablespoons chopped fresh parsley
1	small tomato, chopped and drained
2	teaspoons butter
	Freshly grated Parmesan cheese for sprinkling on top

CHILE SCRAMBLED EGGS
Serves 2

When you are in a hurry for supper, scrambled eggs are satisfying and quick to make. Here, cheese, chiles, and mushrooms are added to make these eggs special. Serve with warm croissants.

In a medium bowl, whisk together eggs, milk, salt, and pepper. Set aside. In a medium skillet over medium heat, melt butter. Add mushrooms and green onions and sauté until tender, about 5 minutes. Stir in chiles. Pour eggs over all and let set for 20 seconds. Stir until light and fluffy and almost dry, about 2 minutes. Add cheese and stir until blended and cheese is melted. Serve with salsa and sour cream, if desired.

4	large eggs
1	tablespoon whole milk
¼	teaspoon salt
	Freshly ground pepper to taste
2	teaspoons butter
2	or 3 medium mushrooms, chopped
2	green onions, including some tender green tops, sliced
2	tablespoons canned chopped green chiles, drained
⅓	cup grated Cheddar cheese
	Fresh Tomato Salsa (page 71) or good-quality purchased tomato salsa for serving (optional)
	Sour cream for serving (optional)

HAM, APPLE, AND CHEESE OMELET
Serves 1

Omelets are fast to make, but they have to be made one at a time. Keep finished omelets warm in a 200ºF oven until all are ready, or serve each one hot as it comes out of the skillet. One omelet can be divided for two people until the next one is ready to serve.

In a small bowl, combine apple, cheese, and ham. Set aside.

In a medium bowl, whisk together eggs, water, salt, and pepper. In an 8-inch omelet pan or nonstick skillet over medium heat, melt butter and swirl to coat bottom of the skillet. When butter foams, pour in egg mixture all at once. Let set until edges begin to cook, about 20 seconds. With a spatula, gently lift edges of mixture and tip the skillet to allow the uncooked egg mixture to flow underneath. Continue to do this until the top is almost dry, 3 to 4 minutes.

Spoon cheese mixture over one half of the omelet. Fold over the other half to cover. Let stand for a few seconds. Turn out onto a warmed plate. Serve immediately.

¼ cup diced peeled apple
¼ cup diced Havarti cheese
¼ cup diced cooked ham
3 large eggs
1 tablespoon water
⅛ teaspoon salt
Freshly ground pepper to taste
1 teaspoon butter

HAM AND CHEESE OMELET

Serves 1

This cheesy omelet with ham makes supper special when served with a Blueberry-Melon Bowl with Honey-Yogurt Dressing (page 62).

In a medium bowl, whisk together eggs, water, salt, and pepper. In an 8-inch omelet pan or nonstick skillet over medium heat, melt butter and swirl to coat bottom of the skillet. When butter foams, add egg mixture all at once. Let set until edges begin to cook, about 20 seconds. With a spatula, gently lift edges of mixture and tip the skillet to allow the uncooked egg mixture to flow underneath. Continue to do this until the top is almost dry, 3 to 4 minutes.

Sprinkle cheeses and ham over one half of the omelet. Fold over the other half to cover. Let stand a few seconds. Turn out onto a warmed plate. Serve immediately.

3   large eggs
1   tablespoon water
⅛   teaspoon salt
    Freshly ground pepper to taste
1   teaspoon butter
¼   cup grated Monterey Jack cheese
¼   cup grated Cheddar cheese
½   cup chopped cooked ham

EGG-SAUSAGE-CHILE BAKE

Serves 4 to 6

Puffy and warm, this casserole is like a soufflé in its homey elegance. Hamburger or ground turkey can be substituted for the sausage.

Preheat oven to 350°F. In a medium skillet over medium heat, combine sausage and onion and sauté, breaking up meat with a spoon, until meat is browned and onions are tender, about 5 minutes. Add salt and pepper. In a lightly sprayed or oiled 8-by-10-inch glass baking dish, arrange half of the chiles. Sprinkle with half of the cheese and spread the meat and onion mixture on top. Arrange remaining chiles on top.

In a medium bowl, whisk together eggs, milk, and flour. Pour over casserole. Add remaining cheese on top. Bake, uncovered, until puffy and firm, about 45 minutes. Let stand for 5 minutes before serving.

1 pound mild bulk sausage
¼ cup chopped yellow onion
½ teaspoon salt
   Freshly ground pepper to taste
1 can (7 ounces) whole green chiles, split lengthwise, seeded, opened flat, and cut into 1-inch squares
1½ cups grated Cheddar cheese
4 large eggs
1½ cups whole milk
¼ cup all-purpose flour

SAUSAGE AND POTATO FRITTATA

Serves 4 to 6

Frittatas are an Italian omelet that has other ingredients mixed with the eggs and is not folded over like the French omelet. They cook slowly on the stove top and then may be finished under the broiler or baked in the oven. This hearty frittata with meat and potatoes is satisfying and filling. Serve with whole-grain toast and jam.

1	large russet potato, peeled and cut into ¾-inch dice
½	pound fresh pork sausage links
¼	cup water
1½	tablespoons vegetable oil
½	cup chopped green onions, including some tender green tops
6	large eggs
2	tablespoons whole milk
½	teaspoon salt
	Freshly ground pepper to taste
1	cup grated Monterey Jack cheese

In a saucepan over high heat, bring just enough lightly salted water to cover potatoes to a boil. Add potatoes, reduce heat to medium, and cook until tender, about 15 minutes. Drain and set aside.

In a large ovenproof skillet over medium heat, combine sausages and water and bring to a boil. Cook for about 10 minutes. Drain sausages and transfer to a plate. Cut into ½-inch slices and set aside. In the same skillet over medium heat, warm oil. Add potatoes, green onions, and sliced sausage and sauté until onions are tender and sausage is browned, 8 to 10 minutes. Spread mixture evenly in the skillet.

Preheat oven to 350°F. In a medium bowl, whisk together eggs, milk, salt, and pepper. Pour over sausage-potato mixture in skillet. Sprinkle with cheese. Bake until eggs are set, about 25 minutes. Let stand for 5 minutes. Cut into wedges and serve from the skillet, or slide the whole frittata onto a warmed plate.

MUSHROOM, BELL PEPPER, AND HAM FRITTATA

Serves 4 to 6

Serve this hearty frittata with hash browns and toasted bagels to a hungry bunch for an easy supper.

In a large ovenproof skillet over medium heat, warm oil. Add onion, bell pepper, and mushrooms and sauté until vegetables are tender, 6 to 7 minutes. Stir in ham and spread mixture evenly in the skillet.

In a medium bowl, whisk together eggs, water, thyme, salt, pepper, 1 cup cheese, and parsley. Pour over ham mixture in skillet. Reduce heat to medium-low, cover, and cook until eggs are set and the top is almost dry, 10 to 12 minutes.

Preheat broiler. Sprinkle remaining ½ cup cheese on top and broil until frittata is puffy and cheese is melted, about 1 minute. Let stand for 5 minutes. Cut into wedges and serve from the skillet, or slide the whole frittata onto a warmed plate. Garnish with a dollop of sour cream and serve.

1 tablespoon vegetable oil

½ cup chopped yellow onion

1 red bell pepper, seeded and chopped

4 ounces mushrooms, sliced

1 cup cubed cooked ham

6 large eggs

2 tablespoons water

¼ teaspoon dried thyme

½ teaspoon salt

Freshly ground pepper to taste

1½ cups grated provolone cheese

¼ cup finely chopped fresh parsley

Sour cream for garnish

BAKED HERBED ZUCCHINI FRITTATA

Serves 6

Bake this light zucchini-studded egg dish in the oven to serve
for a quick supper before an evening at a movie or concert.

Preheat oven to 350°F. In an ovenproof skillet over medium heat, melt butter. Add mushrooms, green onions, and zucchini and sauté until the vegetables are tender, about 5 minutes. Spread mixture evenly in the skillet.

In a medium bowl, whisk together eggs, water, thyme, basil, salt, and pepper. Pour over vegetables in skillet. Sprinkle with the cheeses. Bake until firm, about 30 minutes. Let stand for 5 minutes before serving.

2	tablespoons butter
4	ounces mushrooms, sliced
2	green onions, including some tender green tops, sliced
1	zucchini, unpeeled, chopped
6	large eggs
2	tablespoons water
¼	teaspoon dried thyme
¼	teaspoon dried basil
¼	teaspoon salt
	Freshly ground pepper to taste
1	cup grated mozzarella cheese
¼	cup freshly grated Parmesan cheese

CRUSTLESS SPINACH QUICHE

Serves 4 to 6

This flavorful quiche is quick and easy to make because it does not call for a shell. It is wonderful paired with Exotic Fruit Salad (page 61) for a light supper.

In a large bowl, whisk eggs. Add remaining ingredients and mix well. Spread into a lightly sprayed or oiled 9-inch glass pie plate. Bake until set and bubbly, about 55 minutes. Let stand 5 minutes before serving. Cut into wedges to serve.

2 large eggs
1 cup cottage cheese
4 green onions, including some tender green tops, sliced
1 cup grated Monterey Jack cheese
1 cup grated Cheddar cheese
¼ cup (½ stick) butter, melted
¼ cup all-purpose flour
½ teaspoon baking powder
¼ cup whole milk
½ package (5 ounces) frozen spinach, thawed and squeezed dry
¼ teaspoon salt
  Freshly ground pepper to taste
2 or 3 drops Tabasco sauce

ITALIAN VEGGIE EGG DISH

Serves 4 to 6

Serve this healthful dish with toasted whole-wheat English muffins. Any choice of vegetables can be used.

Arrange the vegetables in an even layer in a lightly sprayed or oiled 8-by-10-inch glass baking dish. In a medium bowl, whisk together eggs, cornstarch, ricotta, yogurt, basil, oregano, salt, and pepper. Pour mixture over vegetables. Sprinkle with cheese. Bake until firm, 35 to 40 minutes. Let set for 5 minutes before serving. Cut into squares to serve.

4   cups chopped mixed vegetables such as onions, broccoli, zucchini, mushrooms, bell peppers, and carrots (see Note)

8   large eggs

2   tablespoons cornstarch

1   cup ricotta or cottage cheese

¼   cup plain, nonfat yogurt or sour cream

½   teaspoon dried basil

¼   teaspoon dried oregano

½   teaspoon salt

    Freshly ground pepper to taste

1½ cups grated mozzarella cheese

NOTE: The vegetables will be al dente as cooked in the directions above. If preferred, blanch vegetables for 2 minutes in boiling water before using. Drain well and dry, then proceed as directed.

EGG, HAM, AND CHILE STRATA

Serves 8

Stratas should be assembled several hours ahead or even the night before baking, to allow the bread to absorb the flavors of the custard. Put together this attractive dish in the morning, and supper will be ready to pop in the oven that night. Use dried or day-old bread in making stratas.

Place bread cubes in the bottom of a lightly sprayed or oiled 9-by-13-inch glass baking dish. Scatter ham and green onions over bread cubes and sprinkle with 1 cup cheese.

In a medium bowl, whisk together eggs, milk, mustard, oregano, basil, salt, and pepper. Stir in chiles and pour over ham mixture in dish. Sprinkle with remaining 1 cup cheese. Cover and refrigerate for several hours or overnight. Bring the strata to room temperature before baking.

Preheat oven to 350°F. Bake strata, uncovered, until set, about 50 minutes. Let stand for 10 minutes. Cut into squares and serve with sour cream and salsa, if desired.

2 cups dried bread cubes (about 1 inch) (see Note on facing page)

2 cups cubed cooked ham

4 green onions, including some tender green tops, sliced

2 cups grated Cheddar cheese

6 large eggs

2 cups whole milk

¼ teaspoon ground mustard

¼ teaspoon dried oregano

¼ teaspoon dried basil

½ teaspoon salt

Freshly ground pepper to taste

1 can (4 ounces) diced green chiles, drained

Fresh Tomato Salsa (page 71) or good-quality purchased salsa and sour cream for serving (optional)

NOTE: To dry bread, cut into 1-inch slices and place on a baking sheet in a 300ºF oven for 15 minutes, turning once, or slice and leave on the countertop to air-dry overnight.

VARIATIONS: Substitute crisply cooked chopped bacon for the ham. For a vegetarian strata, substitute 4 ounces (about 2 cups) chopped or sliced mushrooms for the ham.

BASIC WAFFLES WITH VARIATIONS

Makes 4 waffles

Waffles can be served any time of the day, but are especially good for an easy supper if you are short of time to shop or cook. Serve with butter and syrup, jam, or honey. See the suggestions below for exciting variations.

Preheat and lightly oil waffle iron. In a medium bowl, whisk eggs until foamy. Whisk in melted butter and milk. Add remaining ingredients and whisk just until smooth. Pour $3/4$ cup batter into hot waffle iron. Close lid and bake until steam stops and waffle is lightly browned and crisp, 3 to 4 minutes. Remove waffle and serve. Repeat with remaining batter. Serve immediately, with toppings of your choice.

2   large eggs

$1/2$ cup melted butter (1 stick), or vegetable oil

1$3/4$ cups whole milk

2   cups all-purpose flour

1   tablespoon sugar

4   teaspoons baking powder

$1/4$ teaspoon salt

VARIATIONS

Waffles with Ham: Fold $1/2$ cup diced cooked ham into batter.

Cheese Waffles: Fold $1/2$ cup grated Cheddar or Monterey Jack cheese into batter.

Chocolate Waffles: Combine $1/4$ cup unsweetened cocoa powder and $1/4$ cup sugar and fold into batter.

Poppy Seed Waffles: Fold 2 tablespoons poppy seeds into batter.

Cranberry Waffles: Fold $1/2$ cup dried cranberries into batter.

PANCAKE SUPPER

Makes about 8 pancakes

Pancakes make a filling supper and are quick to fix; kids always love this breakfast-for-supper meal. For variety, you can add chopped dried fruit, chopped nuts, chocolate chips, and/or chopped fresh fruit to this basic recipe.

Lightly oil a large griddle or skillet and preheat over medium-high heat. In a medium bowl, whisk the egg. Add remaining ingredients and whisk until smooth. Pour about ¼ cup batter for each pancake onto hot griddle. Cook until lightly browned and bubbles form, about 2 minutes. Turn and cook about 2 minutes longer. Serve immediately.

1	large egg
1	cup all-purpose flour
1	tablespoon baking powder
1	tablespoon firmly packed brown sugar
2	tablespoons vegetable oil
¼	teaspoon salt
1¼	cups whole milk

SEAFOOD

AND

FISH

CHAPTER 8

FAVORITE RECIPES FROM THE SEA

Seafood and fish are good choices for easy suppers, because they cook quickly and are easy to prepare. Today, fresh seafood is available in most parts of the country due to modern refrigeration and fast methods of transportation.

Fish is naturally tender and full of flavor. It is a good source of protein and is known to provide other health benefits. Eating fish at least twice a week is recommended.

There are many types of fish available that will add variety to your menu; a host of subtle flavor experiences are to be had by venturing beyond salmon steaks and whitefish fillets. Fish is very perishable and should be eaten the day of catch or purchase. Store lightly covered in the refrigerator until ready to cook. Seafood and fish are adaptable to all methods of cooking and freeze well. Frozen fish thaws quickly under a slow stream of cool running water.

This chapter boasts a wide assortment of tempting seafood and fish recipes, including Baked Salmon Steaks with Fresh Fruit Salsa (page 150), Sole Amandine with Lemon-Caper Sauce (page 159), Snapper Fillets in Tomato Sauce (page 161), Sautéed Herbed Scallops and Mushrooms (page 166), Sautéed Shrimp with Garlic and White Wine (page 167), and many exciting others.

BAKED SALMON STEAKS WITH FRESH FRUIT SALSA

Serves 4

Salmon is one of the most popular fishes because of its distinctive color, outstanding flavor, and soft texture. It lends itself to many cooking methods, such as grilling, frying, broiling, poaching, or baking. Here, the salmon is baked in the oven until flaky and served with a refreshing fruit salsa. The salsa should be made ahead to allow the flavors to blend.

Preheat oven to 400°F. Place salmon steaks in a lightly sprayed or oiled 9-by-13-inch glass baking dish. In a small bowl, whisk together melted butter, lemon juice, Worcestershire sauce, salt, pepper, paprika, and parsley. Pour over salmon. Bake until fish flakes when tested with a fork, 10 to 12 minutes. Serve with Fresh Fruit Salsa on the side.

4	salmon steaks (about 6 ounces each)
¼	cup (½ stick) butter, melted
	Juice of 1 lemon
1	teaspoon Worcestershire sauce
½	teaspoon salt
	Freshly ground pepper to taste
1	teaspoon paprika
1	tablespoon chopped fresh parsley
	Fresh Fruit Salsa (recipe on facing page)

FRESH FRUIT SALSA

Allow the salsa to stand for at least 15 to 20 minutes or up to a few hours before serving to allow the flavors to blend.

In a medium bowl, combine all ingredients. Drain if needed before serving. Serve at room temperature.

Makes about 2 cups

NOTE: Those with sensitive skin should wear latex gloves when working with chiles or wash hands thoroughly. Do not touch eyes.

1	papaya, peeled, seeded, and cut into ½-inch cubes
1	cup fresh pineapple, cut into bite-sized pieces and drained
1	fresh jalapeño chile, seeded and finely chopped
¼	cup chopped red onion
1	garlic clove, minced
¼	cup chopped fresh cilantro or parsley
2	teaspoons red wine vinegar
¼	teaspoon salt
	Grated zest of ½ lime
	Juice of 1 lime

BAKED SALMON AND PEAS

Serves 4

A coating of mayonnaise keeps these salmon steaks moist and flavorful as they bake. A border of bright green peas adds color and eye appeal. This is a simple and easy way to prepare this premier fish.

Preheat oven to 400°F. In a small bowl, whisk together mayonnaise, mustard, tarragon, parsley, lemon juice, salt, and pepper.

Spread a thin layer of the mayonnaise mixture on the bottom of a 9-by-13-inch glass baking dish. Arrange salmon in a single layer on top. Spread remaining mayonnaise mixture on top of the salmon. Bake, uncovered, for 8 minutes. Sprinkle peas around the edge of the dish. Bake until fish flakes when tested with a fork and peas are tender, 5 to 6 minutes longer. Garnish with lemon wedges.

½ cup mayonnaise
1 tablespoon Dijon mustard
½ teaspoon dried tarragon
1 tablespoon chopped fresh parsley
1 tablespoon fresh lemon juice
½ teaspoon salt
Freshly ground pepper to taste
4 salmon steaks (about 6 ounces each)
1½ cups fresh peas or frozen peas, rinsed
Lemon wedges for garnish

SKILLET SALMON WITH SPINACH

Serves 4

This combination of sautéed salmon, spinach, garlic, onions, and pasta goes together quickly and should be served immediately. Just a simple green salad will complete this supper.

In a large skillet over medium heat, warm oil. Add salmon and garlic and sauté until salmon turns pink, 3 to 4 minutes. Stir in green onions, spinach, wine, lemon juice, pasta, salt, and pepper. Simmer a few minutes to allow flavors to blend. Serve immediately.

1   tablespoon vegetable oil

1   pound fresh salmon fillet, skin removed, cut into ¾-inch pieces

2   garlic cloves, minced

6   green onions, including some tender green tops, sliced

1   package (10 ounces) frozen spinach, thawed and squeezed dry

¼   cup dry white wine

     Juice of 1 lemon

1   cup rotini, cooked according to package directions and drained

½   teaspoon salt

     Freshly ground pepper to taste

BROILED HALIBUT STEAKS WITH LEMON-WINE-SOY BASTE

Serves 4

Broiling is a simple fast-fix way to prepare fish, but you must watch carefully to prevent overcooking. Here a lively baste adds flavor to the mild, sweet halibut as it broils. Serve with Sautéed Spinach, Garlic, and Mushrooms (page 223). The halibut can also be grilled.

Preheat broiler. Place halibut steaks on an aluminum foil–lined broiler pan. Season generously with salt and pepper and brush with baste. Broil 4 inches from heat for 5 minutes. Turn steaks and brush with baste on the other side. Broil until fish flakes when tested with a fork, about 4 minutes longer. Garnish with parsley.

2 large halibut steaks, 1 inch thick (1½ to 1¾ pounds)
   Salt and freshly ground pepper to taste
   Lemon-Wine-Soy Baste (recipe follows)
   Fresh parsley sprigs for garnish

LEMON-WINE-SOY BASTE

In a small bowl, whisk together all ingredients.

Makes about ¼ cup

2 tablespoons butter, melted
2 tablespoons fresh lemon juice
2 tablespoons soy sauce
½ teaspoon salt

HALIBUT WITH TANGY YOGURT TOPPING

Serves 4

The tangy yogurt sauce adds flavor and keeps the fish moist as it bakes. This recipe is so easy, you won't believe how good it is. Add a Spinach Waldorf Salad (page 52) for contrasting flavors.

Preheat oven to 400°F. In a lightly sprayed or oiled 8-by-10-inch glass baking dish, place fish skin side down. In a small bowl, mix together remaining ingredients except parsley and lemon wedges. Spread the yogurt mixture on top of the fish. Bake until fish turns opaque and flakes when tested with a fork, 12 to 15 minutes. Remove fish from the skin and transfer to plates. Garnish with parsley and lemon wedges. Serve any remaining sauce on the side.

1½ pounds halibut fillets (1 to 1½ inches thick)
1 cup plain nonfat yogurt
2 garlic cloves, minced
1 teaspoon Dijon mustard
2 tablespoons fresh lemon juice
¼ teaspoon salt
Fresh parsley sprigs for garnish
Lemon wedges for garnish

HALIBUT WITH HONEY-ORANGE GLAZE

Serves 4

Mild-flavored halibut is enhanced with a sweet-tart glaze and garnished with orange slices. Serve with acini di pepe (a tiny round pasta) and Spinach and Avocado Salad with Dried Cranberries, Candied Walnuts, and Blue Cheese (page 48).

Preheat oven to 350°F. Place halibut steaks in a lightly sprayed or oiled 9-by-13-inch glass baking dish. Season generously with salt and pepper. In a small bowl, whisk together honey, mustard, marmalade, soy sauce, and wine. Spread on top of the fish. Bake, uncovered, until fish flakes when tested with a fork, about 10 minutes. Serve with acini di pepe, garnished with orange segments.

4 halibut steaks (4 to 6 ounces each)
  Salt and freshly ground pepper to taste
2 tablespoons honey
2 tablespoons Dijon mustard
2 tablespoons orange marmalade
1 tablespoon soy sauce
1 tablespoon dry white wine
1 cup acini di pepe, cooked according to package directions and drained
  Orange segments for garnish

WHITEFISH AND VEGETABLE GRATIN

Serves 4

A great flavor develops as the fish bakes in wine with a crumb-cheese topping. Use thin fish fillets for this dish. Serve with a Romaine, Arugula, and Avocado Salad with Creamy Garlic-Herb Buttermilk Dressing (page 53).

Preheat oven to 400°F. Arrange onion slices in a lightly sprayed or oiled 9-by-13-inch glass baking dish. Place fillets on top and sprinkle with basil and salt and pepper. Arrange mushrooms on top of fish, then tomato slices. Pour wine over all.

In a small bowl, toss bread crumbs with melted butter. Spread on top of fillets and sprinkle with Parmesan. Bake, uncovered, until fish flakes when tested with a fork, 10 to 15 minutes.

1	large yellow onion, sliced and separated into rings
1½	pounds whitefish fillets such as snapper, cod, or sole
¼	teaspoon dried basil
	Salt and freshly ground pepper to taste
3	ounces mushrooms, sliced
1	tomato, sliced
⅓	cup dry white wine
¾	cup dried bread crumbs
¼	cup (½ stick) butter, melted
¼	cup freshly grated Parmesan cheese

BAKED SOLE IN DILL-BUTTER SAUCE ON SPINACH WITH HAZELNUTS

Serves 6

Baked sole in a dill sauce served on a bed of spinach is a delightful supper entrée. Follow with Fresh Pear Upside-Down Cake (page 306) for dessert.

Preheat oven to 400°F. Place fillets in a lightly sprayed or oiled 9-by-13-inch glass baking dish. Season generously with salt and pepper. In a small saucepan over medium heat, combine butter, wine, lemon juice, parsley, dill, and thyme and stir until butter is melted. Pour over fish and bake until fish flakes when tested with a fork, about 10 minutes.

Meanwhile, in a large saucepan over medium heat, cook spinach in 2 tablespoons of water, covered, tossing several times, until wilted, about 5 minutes. Drain well, season with salt and pepper to taste, and keep warm.

Remove fish from the oven. Pour baking liquid from fish into a small saucepan and boil over high heat until liquid is reduced and slightly thickened, about 2 minutes. Arrange spinach on a platter and place the fillets on top. Pour sauce over the fish and spinach and sprinkle with hazelnuts. Serve immediately.

6   sole fillets (4 to 6 ounces each)
    Salt and freshly ground pepper to taste
¼   cup (½ stick) butter
½   cup dry white wine
1   tablespoon fresh lemon juice
1   tablespoon chopped fresh parsley
1   tablespoon chopped fresh dill or ½ teaspoon dried dill
¼   teaspoon dried thyme
1   bag (10 ounces) spinach leaves, rinsed
¼   cup hazelnuts, toasted (see Note) and chopped

NOTE: To toast hazelnuts, place nuts on a baking sheet in a 350°F oven and bake until lightly browned, 10 to 12 minutes. Wrap in a clean, rough towel and rub nuts together to remove most of the skins.

SOLE AMANDINE WITH LEMON-CAPER SAUCE

Serves 4

Sole has delicate, sweet-flavored flesh with a fine, even texture. It can be prepared in a variety of ways, including poaching, steaming, frying, baking, and broiling. Here it is baked in a coating of nuts and bread crumbs and served with a light sauce of lemon and capers. Asparagus makes a nice vegetable accompaniment.

Preheat oven to 400°F. On a large piece of waxed paper combine bread crumbs, almonds, and salt. Pour melted butter into a shallow dish. Dip fillets in butter and then in bread crumb mixture to coat evenly. Place in a lightly sprayed or oiled 8-by-10-inch glass baking dish. Bake until fish flakes when tested with a fork, 12 to 15 minutes. Pour Lemon-Caper Sauce over fish. Garnish with lemon slices and parsley sprigs.

⅓ cup fine dried bread crumbs
¼ cup finely chopped almonds
½ teaspoon salt
¼ cup (½ stick) butter, melted
4 sole fillets (about 6 ounces each)
Lemon-Caper Sauce (recipe follows)
1 lemon, sliced
Fresh parsley sprigs for garnish

LEMON-CAPER SAUCE

In a small pan over medium heat, melt butter. Add capers, lemon juice, parsley, and white pepper and stir until flavors are blended and sauce is warm, about 1 minute.

Makes about ½ cup

¼ cup (½ stick) butter
1½ tablespoons capers, drained
3 tablespoons fresh lemon juice
2 tablespoons finely chopped fresh parsley
Dash of white pepper

BAKED SNAPPER
WITH SOUR CREAM TOPPING
Serves 6

There are many species of snapper, but the best known and most popular is the red snapper. It is so named because it has a reddish-pink skin, red eyes, and a firm flesh. It is suitable for almost any type of preparation. Here it is marinated briefly in wine and then baked with a creamy topping.

Place fillets in a 9-by-13-inch glass baking dish. Pour wine over fish and sprinkle with salt. Let stand for 15 minutes. Drain and discard marinade.

Preheat oven to 400°F. In a medium bowl, mix together mayonnaise, sour cream, mustard, and green onions. Spread mayonnaise mixture over the fish in the baking dish. Sprinkle bread crumbs and cheese on top. Bake until fish flakes when tested with a fork and bread crumbs are toasted, 10 to 15 minutes. Serve with lemon wedges.

2   pounds snapper fillets
½   cup dry white wine
1   teaspoon salt
1   cup mayonnaise
½   cup sour cream
1   teaspoon Dijon mustard
3   or 4 green onions, including some tender green tops, sliced
    Dried bread crumbs for sprinkling on top
    Parmesan for sprinkling on top
    Lemon wedges for garnish

SNAPPER FILLETS IN TOMATO SAUCE

Serves 6

Baking is one of the easiest ways to prepare fish. Here the snapper simmers in the oven cloaked in a seasoned tomato sauce and topped with cheese. Serve with Onion Rice (page 197).

Preheat oven to 400° F. Place fillets in a lightly sprayed or oiled 8-by-10-inch glass baking dish. Season generously with salt and pepper. In a medium skillet over medium heat, warm oil. Add onion and garlic and sauté until tender, about 5 minutes. Add tomato sauce, oregano, and basil and simmer 1 to 2 minutes. Pour sauce over the fish and sprinkle with cheese. Bake, uncovered, until fish flakes when tested with a fork, about 20 minutes.

1½ to 2 pounds snapper fillets
Salt and freshly ground pepper to taste
1 tablespoon vegetable oil
½ cup chopped yellow onion
1 garlic clove, minced
1 can (8 ounces) tomato sauce
¼ teaspoon dried oregano
¼ teaspoon dried basil
1 cup grated mozzarella cheese

SOY SNAPPER

Serves 4

Snapper is a fairly inexpensive fish, but it's full of flavor and usually available year-round. Fried Rice (page 198) is a complementary side dish to this entrée.

Place fillets in a lightly sprayed or oiled 8-by-10-inch glass baking dish. Season generously with salt and pepper. In a small bowl, mix together the juice from 1 lemon, soy sauce, ginger, oil, thyme, and garlic. Pour over fish. Let stand 15 minutes at room temperature.

Preheat broiler. Remove fish from marinade and discard marinade. Place fish on an aluminum foil–lined broiler pan and broil 4 inches from the heat until fish flakes when tested with a fork, 4 to 5 minutes on each side. Transfer to a platter and arrange lemon slices on top of fish. Sprinkle with parsley and serve immediately.

1½ pounds red snapper fillets
    Salt and freshly ground pepper to taste
2   lemons, 1 juiced and 1 sliced
3   tablespoons soy sauce
½   teaspoon ground ginger
1   tablespoon vegetable oil
½   teaspoon dried thyme
2   garlic cloves, minced
¼   cup chopped fresh parsley

PAN-SEARED RARE AHI
WITH WASABI CREAM
Serves 4

Ahi (also called yellowfin) is a firm, dark red tuna, rich in oils and flavor, but special care must be taken not to overcook; its fine quality is best demonstrated when eaten rare. In this gourmet classic, the tuna is seared quickly on the outside and kept nearly raw on the inside. The Wasabi Cream adds a sharp, fiery flavor similar to horseradish to this delicate fish. Wasabi is available in paste or powder form. Use it sparingly, as it is quite hot. You'll like Fried Rice (page 198) with this dish.

In a small bowl, mix together butter, pepper, flour, and salt. Spread half of the butter mixture on one side of the tuna. In a heavy skillet (preferably cast iron) over medium-high heat, warm olive oil until hot, but not smoking. Add tuna, coated side down, and cook, 1½ to 2 minutes. Spread remaining butter mixture on top and turn. Cook until browned, 1½ to 2 minutes longer for rare. (For medium-rare, cook about 4 minutes on each side.) Serve immediately with Wasabi Cream.

¼ cup (½ stick) butter, at room temperature
1 teaspoon cracked black pepper
1 tablespoon all-purpose flour
1 teaspoon coarse salt
1½ to 2 pounds ahi tuna steak, 1 inch thick
1½ tablespoons olive oil
Wasabi Cream (recipe follows)

WASABI CREAM

In a small bowl, mix together all ingredients.

Makes about ½ cup

½ cup sour cream or plain nonfat yogurt
½ teaspoon wasabi paste, or more to taste
¼ teaspoon soy sauce

CRAB CAKES WITH ROASTED RED BELL PEPPER AIOLI

Serves 4

Crab is so versatile it can be used in soups, stews, salads, casseroles, and sandwiches. For a real treat, serve these outstanding crab cakes topped with a garlicky red pepper mayonnaise on a bed of greens. The aioli is also excellent on sandwiches, salads, and vegetables.

In a medium bowl, whisk the egg. Add crabmeat, green onions, bread crumbs, parsley, mayonnaise, mustard, Worcestershire sauce, Tabasco, salt, and pepper and mix thoroughly. Refrigerate 30 minutes. Form mixture into 8 cakes about ½ inch thick.

In a large skillet over medium-high heat, warm 2 tablespoons oil. Working in batches, fry 4 cakes until lightly browned, 4 to 5 minutes on each side. Transfer to a plate and keep warm. Add more oil, if needed, and fry remaining cakes. Serve immediately on greens with Roasted Red Bell Pepper Aioli, garnished with lemon wedges.

1	large egg
1	pound lump crabmeat, picked over and flaked
3	green onions, including some tender green tops, finely chopped
1	cup coarse dried sourdough bread crumbs
¼	cup finely chopped fresh parsley
¼	cup mayonnaise
2	teaspoons Dijon mustard
1	teaspoon Worcestershire sauce
	Dash of Tabasco sauce
¼	teaspoon salt
	Freshly ground pepper to taste
2	to 3 tablespoons vegetable oil
4	to 5 cups mixed salad greens or baby spinach
	Roasted Red Bell Pepper Aioli (recipe on facing page)
1	lemon, cut into wedges

ROASTED RED BELL PEPPER AIOLI

In a food processor, process roasted pepper and garlic until finely chopped, then add remaining ingredients and process until smooth. Serve at room temperature.

Makes about 1 cup

1	roasted red bell pepper (see Note, page 74), coarsely chopped, or 1 jar (7 ounces) roasted red bell peppers, rinsed, drained, patted dry, and coarsely chopped
2	garlic cloves, coarsely chopped
2	teaspoons red wine vinegar
2	to 3 drops Tabasco sauce
1/4	teaspoon salt
1	cup mayonnaise

SAUTÉED HERBED SCALLOPS AND MUSHROOMS

Serves 4

Scallops are a popular mollusk with a sweet taste and moist, tender flesh. There are two main types: small bay scallops and large sea scallops. In this preparation, the scallops are sautéed with mushrooms in a buttery herb and wine sauce for a quick, elegant dish. Serve with baguette slices.

In a medium skillet over medium heat, melt butter. Add garlic and mushrooms and sauté for 2 minutes. Add scallops and sauté until they turn opaque, 4 to 5 minutes longer. Transfer scallops, garlic, and mushrooms to a plate. Add wine, salt, thyme, basil, and oregano to the skillet. Raise heat to high and boil until liquid is reduced by half, about 1 minute. Reduce heat to medium and return scallops and mushrooms to the pan. Stir until reheated. Serve sprinkled with chopped parsley.

2	tablespoons butter
2	garlic cloves, minced
8	ounces mushrooms, sliced
1	pound sea scallops, muscle removed (see Note)
¼	cup dry white wine
¼	teaspoon salt
¼	teaspoon dried thyme
¼	teaspoon dried basil
¼	teaspoon dried oregano
	Chopped fresh parsley for garnish

NOTE: The abductor muscle at the side of the scallop hinges the two shells together. It is edible, but may be tough. To remove, cut away with a knife.

SAUTÉED SHRIMP WITH GARLIC AND WHITE WINE

Serves 4

Succulent shrimp sautéed in garlic butter makes a quick supper dish. Serve with Spinach with Bacon and Egg Topping (page 222).

In a large skillet over medium heat, melt butter. Add garlic and sauté 2 minutes. Add shrimp and sauté until shrimp turns pink, 2 to 3 minutes longer. Season with salt and pepper and transfer to a warmed serving platter.

Add wine and lemon juice to skillet, bring to a boil, and boil 30 seconds. Reduce heat, return shrimp to the pan, add chopped parsley, and stir until heated through. Transfer to a serving platter, garnish with parsley sprigs, and serve immediately.

¼ cup (½ stick) butter

3 garlic cloves, finely chopped

1¼ pounds large or jumbo shrimp, peeled and deveined

¼ teaspoon salt
   Freshly ground pepper to taste

¼ cup dry white wine

2 tablespoons fresh lemon juice

3 tablespoons chopped fresh parsley, plus fresh parsley sprigs for garnish

STEAMER CLAMS

Serves 4

This popular shellfish is steamed in a flavorful broth, then served in bowls along with the cooking liquid. Serve with baguette slices for dipping in the broth and melted butter.

In a large bowl, combine clams, salt, and cornmeal and add cold water to cover. Let stand for 1 hour. Drain and rinse thoroughly several times to remove any sand.

In a large pot over high heat, combine broth, wine, garlic, bay leaf, parsley, and seasonings and bring to a boil. Add clams, reduce heat to low, and simmer, covered, stirring once, until shells open, 5 to 6 minutes. Discard any unopened clams. Divide clams among individual bowls. Strain broth through a fine-mesh sieve and pour over clams. Serve with melted butter in small bowls on the side for dipping.

4   dozen fresh littleneck clams in the shell, well scrubbed

1   tablespoon salt

1   tablespoon cornmeal

2   cups chicken broth

¼   cup dry white wine

2   garlic cloves, split

1   bay leaf

2   fresh parsley sprigs

¼   teaspoon dried oregano

¼   teaspoon dried basil

    Salt and freshly ground pepper to taste

1   cup (2 sticks) butter, melted

SALMON LOAF

Serves 4 to 6

For convenience, this recipe calls for canned salmon, but fresh, cooked salmon can be used, if available. Bake potatoes along with the salmon loaf for an easy supper. The Lemon-Dill Mayonnaise adds a refreshing accent.

Preheat oven to 350°F. In a medium bowl, mix together all ingredients except Lemon-Dill Mayonnaise. Spoon into a lightly sprayed or oiled 5-by-8-by-3-inch loaf pan and bake until firm, about 1 hour. Let stand for 5 minutes. Remove from pan and slice to serve. Pass the Lemon-Dill Mayonnaise in a small bowl.

1	can (15½ ounces) boneless and skinless pink salmon, drained (about 2 cups)
1	cup crushed saltines (about 20)
¼	cup chopped yellow onion
1	large egg
¼	cup whole milk
1	tablespoon fresh lemon juice
1	teaspoon grated lemon zest
1	teaspoon dried dill
¼	teaspoon salt
1	teaspoon Worcestershire sauce
	Lemon-Dill Mayonnaise (recipe follows; optional)

LEMON-DILL MAYONNAISE

In a small bowl, mix together all ingredients.

Makes about 1 cup

¾	cup mayonnaise
2	tablespoons fresh lemon juice
1	teaspoon grated lemon zest
½	teaspoon dried dill
¼	teaspoon sugar

MAIN-COURSE PASTA

GRAINS AND LEGUMES

CHAPTER 9

SATISFYING AND FILLING ENTRÉES

Main-course pasta, grain, and legume dishes that include meat, poultry, or seafood are popular homemade options for easy suppers and are suitable for a full meal. For convenience, keep the following dried staples in your pantry.

Pasta is a term used to describe a wide variety of noodles made from dough. It comes in many sizes, shapes, colors, and thicknesses. It is sold dry in packages or boxes or in bulk at most supermarkets, as well as fresh at some specialty food stores and Italian markets. Dried pasta will keep indefinitely, but fresh pasta should be refrigerated and used as soon as possible or frozen up to a month. Pasta serves as a foundation for sauces, casseroles, and salads. Almost every country has some form of pasta.

Pasta should be cooked in lots of salted boiling water just until al dente (pleasantly firm to bite), not soft. Follow package directions and do not overcook.

There are many varieties of rice; the most commonly used are white and brown. Brown rice is the entire grain with only the outer husk removed and so has fiber-rich health advantages. White rice has had the husk, bran, and germ removed. Arborio, a short-grained rice with a high starch content, is traditionally used in risotto, the classic Italian rice dish known for its creamy texture. Rice is popular to use in casseroles combined with other ingredients. Remember that rice triples in volume when cooked. Follow the cooking directions on the package.

Some of the more popular legumes are beans, lentils, peanuts, peas, and soybeans. They are high in protein and contain some vitamin B, carbohydrates, fat, and minerals. They are pleasantly filling and are often used in vegetarian dishes as a main course.

This chapter employs these wholesome ingredients combined with meat, poultry, and seafood in main dishes such as Shrimp and Curry Pasta (page 179), Ready Spaghetti (page 174), Chicken Florentine (page 183), Shrimp and Rice (page 185), Chicken and Rice Pilaf (page 182), and Beef, Beans, and Rice Casserole (page 186).

HAMBURGER-MACARONI-TOMATO CASSEROLE

Serves 6

This family dish can be made in the morning and baked later for supper. Include a Romaine, Arugula, and Avocado Salad with Creamy Garlic-Herb Buttermilk Dressing (page 53) and Double Chocolate Ice Cream Sundaes (page 321) to round out the menu.

Preheat oven to 350°F. Place macaroni in a lightly sprayed or oiled 2-quart casserole. In a large skillet over medium heat, combine beef, onion, and bell pepper and sauté, breaking up meat with a spoon, until meat is browned and vegetables are tender, 6 to 7 minutes, adding a little oil if needed. Stir in tomato sauce, basil, salt, and pepper. Add to the casserole and mix well. Bake, covered, for 35 minutes. Uncover and stir. Sprinkle with cheese and bake, uncovered, until bubbly and cheese is melted, about 10 minutes longer.

6	ounces (2 cups) large elbow macaroni, cooked according to package directions and drained
1	pound ground beef
½	cup chopped yellow onion
½	cup chopped green or red bell pepper
	Vegetable oil, as needed
1	can (15 ounces) tomato sauce
½	teaspoon dried basil
¼	teaspoon salt
	Freshly ground pepper to taste
1	cup grated Cheddar cheese

READY SPAGHETTI

Serves 6

This sauce can be served almost immediately, but the longer it simmers, the better it gets. Serve with garlic bread and Tossed Green Salad with Italian Dressing (page 50).

In a large skillet over medium heat, combine beef, onion, and garlic and sauté, breaking up the meat with a spoon, until meat is browned and vegetables are tender, 6 to 7 minutes, adding a little oil if needed. Add tomatoes, tomato sauce, wine, basil, oregano, sugar, salt, and pepper and simmer, uncovered, until flavors are blended, 10 to 20 minutes. Serve over spaghetti, sprinkled with Parmesan.

1	pound ground beef
½	cup chopped yellow onion
2	garlic cloves, minced
	Vegetable oil, as needed
1	can (14½ ounces) crushed tomatoes in thick purée
1	can (14½ ounces) diced or ready-cut Italian-recipe tomatoes
1	can (8 ounces) tomato sauce
½	cup dry red wine
½	teaspoon dried basil
½	teaspoon dried oregano
½	teaspoon sugar
¾	teaspoon salt
	Freshly ground pepper to taste
12	ounces spaghetti, cooked according to package directions and drained
	Freshly grated Parmesan cheese for sprinkling on top

CHICKEN AND TOMATO SAUCE WITH BASIL AND PINE NUTS ON PASTA

Serves 4

This thick sauce served over pasta is the centerpiece for a great meal. Just heat all the ingredients together and supper is ready. Havarti cheese is a semisoft Danish cheese, mild and mellow.

In a medium saucepan over medium heat, combine all ingredients except cheeses and pasta. Simmer, uncovered, 5 minutes. Add Havarti cheese and stir until melted, about 1 minute. Serve over pasta, sprinkled with Parmesan.

1	can (14½ ounces) crushed tomatoes in thick purée
¼	cup chicken broth
2	cups cubed cooked chicken breast (see Note, page 30)
2	tablespoons pine nuts, toasted (see Note, page 206)
½	cup chopped fresh basil or 1 teaspoon dried basil
2	tablespoons chopped fresh parsley
½	teaspoon salt
	Freshly ground pepper to taste
1	cup grated Havarti cheese
	Parmesan cheese for sprinkling on top
8	ounces (2 cups) penne pasta or other dried pasta, cooked according to package directions and drained

PASTA WITH CHICKEN, ZUCCHINI, AND MUSHROOMS IN QUICK TOMATO SAUCE

Serves 4 to 6

Enjoy this one-dish meal after a busy workday. For quick assembling, cook the chicken ahead of time. End the meal with Double Chocolate Ice Cream Sundaes (page 321).

Preheat oven to 350°F. Place zucchini and mushrooms in a lightly sprayed or oiled 2-quart casserole. Add chicken, tomato sauce, pasta, salt, and pepper and mix well. Cover and bake until bubbly, about 40 minutes. Sprinkle with cheese and bake, uncovered, until cheese is melted, about 5 minutes longer.

1   zucchini, unpeeled, halved lengthwise and cut into ½-inch slices (about 2 cups)

4   ounces mushrooms, quartered

2   cups cubed cooked chicken breast (see Note, page 30)

2   cups Quick Tomato Sauce (recipe follows)

8   ounces (2½ cups) ziti, cooked according to package directions and drained

¼   teaspoon salt
    Freshly ground pepper to taste

1   cup grated mozzarella cheese

QUICK TOMATO SAUCE

In a small saucepan over medium heat, combine all ingredients. Simmer, uncovered, stirring occasionally, until flavors are blended, 5 to 10 minutes.

Makes about 2 cups

1   can (15 ounces) tomato sauce

1   garlic clove, minced

½   teaspoon dried oregano

½   teaspoon dried basil

¼   teaspoon salt
     Freshly ground pepper to taste

FETTUCCINI WITH CHICKEN, SPINACH, AND PARMESAN CHEESE SAUCE

Serves 4

Fettuccini is a flat strand pasta. Here it is combined with chicken and spinach and a cheese sauce for an all-time favorite supper. Serve with a Summer Salad Bowl (page 57).

Return fettuccini to cooking pan over low heat. Stir in chicken and spinach. Add hot cheese sauce and toss several minutes until flavors are blended. Season with salt and pepper and serve immediately.

8 ounces fettuccini, cooked according to package directions and drained

2 cups cubed cooked chicken breast (see Note, page 30)

½ package (5 ounces) frozen spinach, thawed and squeezed dry

Parmesan Cheese Sauce (recipe follows)

Salt and freshly ground pepper to taste

PARMESAN CHEESE SAUCE

In a medium saucepan over medium heat, melt butter. Add flour and stir until bubbly. Add milk and broth and stir until smooth and thickened, about 2 minutes. Add Parmesan, wine (if using), salt, and white pepper and stir until cheese is melted, about 1 minute longer. Remove from heat and stir in sour cream. Serve immediately.

Makes about 1½ cups

2 tablespoons butter

2 tablespoons all-purpose flour

1 cup whole milk

¼ cup chicken broth

¼ cup freshly grated Parmesan cheese

1 tablespoon dry white wine (optional)

¼ teaspoon salt

Pinch of white pepper

½ cup sour cream

FAMILY NIGHT LAMB AND NOODLES

Serves 6 to 8

When our families get together with us for supper, it is hard to find a dish that everyone likes. This is one that gets everyone's approval, even the teenagers.

Preheat oven to 350°F. In a skillet over medium heat, combine lamb, onion, garlic, and celery and sauté, breaking up meat with a spoon, until meat is browned and vegetables are tender, about 5 minutes, adding a little oil if needed. Stir in tomato sauce. Reduce heat to medium-low and simmer, uncovered, for 10 to 15 minutes, stirring several times.

Place noodles in a lightly sprayed or oiled 2-quart casserole. Add lamb mixture and mix well. Sprinkle cheese on top. Bake, uncovered, until bubbly and cheese is melted, about 35 minutes.

1½ pounds ground lamb

1 cup chopped yellow onion

2 garlic cloves, minced

3 celery stalks, cut on the diagonal into ½-inch slices

Vegetable oil, as needed

3 cups tomato sauce

6 ounces (2 cups) egg noodles, cooked according to package directions and drained

1½ cups grated Cheddar cheese

SHRIMP AND CURRY PASTA

Serves 4

This light pasta supper relies on spices for flavor instead of a rich sauce. Peas mingled with shrimp add contrast and color. This entrée only takes a short time to prepare.

In a large skillet over medium heat, melt 1 tablespoon butter. Add onion and sauté until tender, about 5 minutes. Stir in curry powder, cumin, salt, and red pepper flakes. Add tomato and cook for 5 minutes. Add pasta, peas, shrimp, parsley, and remaining 2 tablespoons butter and mix well. Cook until heated through, about 5 minutes longer, stirring occasionally. Serve immediately.

2	to 3 tablespoons butter
1	cup chopped yellow onion
1	teaspoon curry powder
1/2	teaspoon ground cumin
1/2	teaspoon salt
1/8	teaspoon crushed red pepper flakes
1	large tomato, seeded (see Note), chopped, and drained
8	ounces (2 cups) penne, cooked according to package directions and drained
1	cup fresh or frozen peas
1/2	pound small cooked bay shrimp
1/4	cup chopped fresh parsley

NOTE: To seed tomatoes, cut tomato in half and gently squeeze the halves over the sink and scrape out the seeds with a spoon or your finger.

SEASIDE CASSEROLE

Serves 4 to 6

In this casserole, crab and shrimp are enhanced with a creamy sauce of cheeses and sour cream mixed with shell pasta to carry out the seaworthy theme. Serve this elegant dish with melon slices and clusters of grapes alongside.

Preheat oven to 350°F. In a food processor or blender, combine cream cheese, sour cream, and cottage cheese and process until smooth.

In a lightly sprayed or oiled 2-quart casserole, toss together pasta, green onions, salt, white pepper, shrimp, crabmeat, and mushrooms. Add cheese mixture and mix well. Cover and bake until bubbly, about 45 minutes. Stir before serving and garnish with melons and grapes.

8 ounces cream cheese, at room temperature, cut up

1/2 cup sour cream

3/4 cup cottage cheese

8 ounces (2 3/4 cups) large shell pasta, cooked according to package directions and drained

6 green onions, including some tender green tops, sliced

1/4 teaspoon salt

1/8 teaspoon white pepper

1/2 pound cooked small bay shrimp

1/2 pound lump crabmeat, picked over and flaked

8 ounces mushrooms, sliced

Melon slices and grape clusters for garnish

LINGUINE WITH CLAM SAUCE

Serves 4

For easy assembling, canned clams are used in this quick sauce tossed with linguine. Linguine is a long, narrow, flat noodle that cooks quickly.

In a small saucepan over medium heat, warm olive oil. Add garlic and sauté for 1 minute. Stir in red pepper flakes, salt, and reserved clam juice. Cook for 2 minutes. Add clams and parsley to sauce and cook until clams are heated through and flavors are blended, about 5 minutes. Toss with hot linguine and serve immediately.

3 tablespoons olive oil

2 garlic cloves, finely chopped

1/8 teaspoon crushed red pepper flakes, or to taste

1/4 teaspoon salt

3 cans (6 1/2 ounces each) chopped clams, drained (reserve juice)

2 tablespoons chopped fresh parsley

8 ounces fresh linguine, cooked according to package directions and drained

CHICKEN AND RICE PILAF

Serves 4

For a low-fat, nutritious meal, try this chicken and rice dish. It is a good way to use leftover chicken or turkey. Serve with Blueberry-Melon Bowl with Honey-Yogurt Dressing (page 62).

Preheat oven to 350°F. In a medium skillet over medium heat, melt butter. Add onion and mushrooms and sauté until tender, about 5 minutes. Stir in rice. Add broth, salt, and pepper and stir to combine. Transfer to a lightly sprayed or oiled 2-quart casserole. Add chicken and mix well. Cover and bake until liquid is absorbed and rice is tender, about 45 minutes. Uncover, stir in peas and continue to bake, uncovered, until peas are heated through, about 10 minutes longer.

2   tablespoons butter

½   cup chopped yellow onion

3   ounces mushrooms, sliced

1   cup long-grain white rice

2   cups chicken broth

½   teaspoon salt
    Freshly ground pepper to taste

2   cups cubed cooked chicken (see Note, page 30) or roasted turkey breast

1   cup peas, fresh or frozen

CHICKEN FLORENTINE

Serves 4

Here is a creative one-dish supper combining chicken, rice, and spinach that is nutritious and convenient to prepare. Serve with Exotic Fruit Salad (page 61).

Preheat oven to 350°F. In a large skillet over medium heat, melt butter. Add chicken and onion and sauté until chicken turns opaque and onions are tender, about 5 minutes. Stir in rice. Add broth, spinach, oregano, salt, pepper, and nutmeg and mix well. Transfer to a lightly sprayed or oiled 2-quart casserole and sprinkle with Parmesan. Cover and bake until liquid is absorbed and rice is tender, about 45 minutes.

2	tablespoons butter
2	boned and skinned chicken breast halves (about 1 pound), cut into 1-inch pieces
½	cup chopped yellow onion
¾	cup long-grain white rice
1	can (14 ounces) chicken broth
½	package (5 ounces) frozen spinach, thawed and squeezed dry
½	teaspoon dried oregano
¼	teaspoon salt
	Freshly ground pepper to taste
	Pinch of ground nutmeg
¼	cup freshly grated Parmesan cheese

MEXICAN CHICKEN AND RICE

Serves 4 to 6

This may not seem easy, because there is browning and chopping to do, but once the chicken is in the pot with the rice and sauce, the dish needs no other attention while it bakes to savory perfection. Serve with an Orange, Cucumber, and Red Onion Salad with Lime-Cumin Dressing (page 54) and a basket of warm tortillas.

Preheat oven to 350°F. In a Dutch oven over medium-high heat, warm 1 tablespoon oil. Add chicken and cook until lightly browned, about 5 minutes on each side. Transfer to a plate.

In the same Dutch oven over medium heat, warm remaining ½ tablespoon oil. Add onion, bell pepper, and garlic and sauté until tender, about 5 minutes. Stir in rice. Add tomatoes with juice, broth, salsa, cumin, salt, and pepper and cook for 2 minutes. Return chicken to pot and mix well. Cover and bake until rice is tender and chicken is no longer pink in the center, 45 to 50 minutes.

1½ tablespoons vegetable oil

6 boned and skinned chicken thighs (1½ to 2 pounds)

1 cup chopped yellow onion

½ cup chopped green bell pepper

2 garlic cloves, minced

¾ cup long-grain white rice

1 can (14½ ounces) whole tomatoes, with juice, cut up

1 cup chicken broth

½ cup Fresh Tomato Salsa (page 71) or good-quality purchased tomato salsa

¼ teaspoon ground cumin

¼ teaspoon salt

Freshly ground pepper to taste

SHRIMP AND RICE

Serves 4 to 6

This combination of earthy, nutty-flavored wild rice and mild white rice with shrimp and tomatoes makes a terrific one-dish meal. Wild rice isn't true rice; it is actually a long-grain marsh grass that cooks up in the same manner as rice.

2	tablespoons butter
1	cup chopped yellow onion
1	garlic clove, minced
½	cup wild rice, thoroughly rinsed and drained
2½	cups chicken broth
¼	teaspoon salt
	Freshly ground pepper to taste
½	cup long-grain white rice
¼	cup chopped fresh parsley
1	plum (Roma) tomato, chopped
8	ounces cooked small bay shrimp

Preheat oven to 350°F. In a medium sauce-pan over medium heat, melt butter. Add onion and garlic and sauté until tender, about 5 minutes. Stir in wild rice. Add broth, salt, and pepper. Raise heat to high, bring to a boil, and cook for 1 minute. Stir in white rice. Transfer to a lightly sprayed or oiled 2-quart casserole. Bake, covered, for 45 minutes. Stir in parsley, tomato, and shrimp. Cover and continue baking until liquid is absorbed and rice is tender, about 15 minutes longer.

BEEF, BEANS, AND RICE CASSEROLE

Serves 6

This casserole can be made with or without meat, depending on the menu.
Portable and popular, it's a good dish to take to a potluck supper.

Preheat oven to 350°F. In a large skillet over medium heat, combine beef and onion and sauté, breaking up meat with a spoon, until meat is browned and onions are tender, about 5 minutes, adding a little oil if needed. Transfer to a lightly sprayed or oiled 3-quart casserole. Add remaining ingredients except cheese and mix well.

Bake, covered, for about 1 hour. Uncover and sprinkle cheese evenly over. Continue baking, uncovered, until bubbly and cheese is melted, about 10 minutes.

1	pound ground beef
1	cup chopped yellow onion
	Vegetable oil, as needed
1	package (16 ounces) frozen lima beans, thawed
2	cans (15 ounces each) red kidney beans, drained and rinsed
1	can (15 ounces) garbanzo beans, drained and rinsed
½	cup long-grain white rice, cooked according to package directions
1	cup pitted black olives
1	cup ketchup
¼	cup firmly packed brown sugar
1	teaspoon molasses
1	teaspoon chili powder
1	tablespoon Worcestershire sauce
2	tablespoons cider vinegar
½	teaspoon salt
⅛	teaspoon freshly ground pepper
1	cup grated Cheddar cheese

GOOD CASSEROLE

Serves 6 to 8

Reed's first comment was "Wow, this is good," when he tasted this recipe. It is made in layers and will serve a crowd or be enough for two meals. This is an ideal dish to serve at a family get-together or a casual company supper, along with Best Coleslaw (page 55).

Preheat oven to 350°F. Place noodles while still warm in a lightly sprayed or oiled 3- to 4-quart casserole and toss with butter. In a medium bowl, mix together cream cheese, cottage cheese, sour cream, parsley, salt, and pepper. Spread mixture over the noodles.

In a medium skillet over medium heat, combine beef, onion, and garlic and sauté, breaking up meat with a spoon, until meat is browned and vegetables are tender, 6 to 7 minutes. Add a little oil if needed. Stir in tomato sauce and simmer several minutes. Pour over the noodles and top with cheese; do not mix. Bake, covered, until bubbly, about 35 minutes.

12	ounces (4 cups) egg noodles, cooked according to package directions and drained
2	tablespoons butter, at room temperature
8	ounces cream cheese, at room temperature
1	cup cottage cheese
½	cup sour cream or plain nonfat yogurt
½	cup chopped fresh parsley
¾	teaspoon salt
	Freshly ground pepper to taste
1	pound ground beef
1	cup chopped yellow onion
1	garlic clove, minced
	Vegetable oil, as needed
1	can (15 ounces) tomato sauce
2	cups grated Cheddar cheese

PASTA
GRAIN
AND LEGUME SIDE DISHES

CHAPTER 10

COMPLEMENTARY ACCOMPANIMENTS FOR ANY MEAL

Side dishes are designed to complement the entrée and round out the meal. They add interest and variety. Many of these side dishes are hearty enough to serve as a main course as well. Some of these dishes have been created to go with special entrées and others are at your service to mix and match.

Include some of the following tasty combinations with your easy suppers: Fettuccini with Basil Pesto (page 190), Poppy Seed Noodles (page 193), Parmesan-Pecan Rice (page 195), Double Corn Polenta (page 199), and Fried Rice (page 198).

FETTUCCINI WITH BASIL PESTO

Serves 4

For a fast supper dish that fits into a busy schedule, here is a quick sauce for fettuccini that goes well with Grilled Shrimp (page 292) or other seafood. For dessert, try a refreshing lemon sherbet. Make Basil Pesto in the summer when basil is in season and freeze it in small containers or in ice cube trays for year-round use.

In a small bowl, stir together pesto and sour cream. Toss with fettuccini. Sprinkle with Parmesan and serve immediately.

½   cup Basil Pesto, homemade (recipe follows) or good-quality purchased

½   cup sour cream

9   ounces fettuccini, cooked according to package directions and drained

Freshly grated Parmesan cheese for sprinkling on top

BASIL PESTO

In a food processor or blender, combine all ingredients except olive oil. Process until minced. With motor running, slowly pour olive oil through feed tube and blend until a paste forms. Scrape down sides of bowl as needed with a spatula. Transfer to a bowl, cover, and refrigerate until ready to use, or freeze in an airtight container for up to 6 months.

Makes about ½ cup

2   cups firmly packed basil leaves, rinsed and patted dry

2   fresh parsley sprigs

2   garlic cloves, coarsely chopped

¼   cup pine nuts or chopped walnuts

¼   cup finely grated Parmesan cheese

¼   teaspoon salt

Freshly ground pepper to taste

3   to 4 tablespoons olive oil

ORZO AND CHILES

Serves 4

Orzo is small, oval-shaped pasta that is often interchanged with rice. Here chiles are added for extra flavor. Serve this side with Mexican food.

In a large saucepan over high heat, bring water to a boil. Add orzo, reduce heat to medium, and cook, uncovered, until tender, about 10 minutes. Drain. Add chiles, salt, and pepper. Toss with butter and serve immediately.

6   cups water

1   cup orzo

1   can (4 ounces) chopped green chiles, drained

¼   teaspoon salt

Freshly ground pepper to taste

1   tablespoon butter

ONE-PAN MAC 'N' CHEESE

Serves 4

Here is a simplified version of a perennially family-pleasing cheese dish. The optional blue cheese and diced chiles add a new dimension. A platter of fresh seasonal fruits is a good accompaniment.

Cook macaroni according to package directions and drain. Return macaroni to cooking pot and place over medium heat. Stir in flour. Add milk and mix well. Add salt and pepper. Add cheese and stir until the cheese is melted, about 2 minutes. Add blue cheese and chiles, if using, and mix well. Serve immediately.

8   ounces (2 cups) elbow macaroni
1   tablespoon all-purpose flour
½   cup whole milk
½   teaspoon salt
    Freshly ground pepper to taste
2   cups grated sharp Cheddar cheese
2   tablespoons crumbled blue cheese (optional)
1   can (4 ounces) chopped green chiles, drained (optional)

POPPY SEED NOODLES

Serves 4 to 6

Make this simple pasta dish studded with poppy seeds to go with chicken or meat. Poppy seed is the dried seed of the poppy plant—it has a crunchy texture and nutty flavor.

Place noodles in a large, warmed bowl. Add butter, salt, pepper, and poppy seeds and toss gently. Serve immediately.

6 ounces (2 cups) egg noodles, cooked according to package directions and drained

2 tablespoons butter

¼ teaspoon salt
Freshly ground pepper to taste

1 tablespoon poppy seeds

PASTA, GRAIN, AND LEGUME SIDE DISHES

OVEN BROWN RICE AND VEGETABLES

Serves 4

Brown rice has a chewy texture and a nutlike flavor. It has more nutrients and fiber than white rice because it is the whole grain with only the outer husk removed. Serve with Grilled Salmon Steaks with Dill Sauce (page 287).

Preheat oven to 350°F. Place all ingredients in a lightly sprayed or oiled 2-quart casserole and mix well. Bake, covered, until rice and vegetables are tender and liquid is absorbed, about 1 hour.

1	cup brown rice
1	cup sliced celery
4	ounces mushrooms, sliced
½	cup chopped yellow onion
2	cups chicken or vegetable broth
2	tablespoons soy sauce
1	teaspoon Worcestershire sauce
¼	teaspoon salt
	Freshly ground pepper to taste

PARMESAN-PECAN RICE
Serves 4

Many entrées call for a complementary side dish that is flavorful but not highly seasoned, such as this one. It is easy to make and can be served with almost any main course. Pecans are added for extra crunch and flavor.

In a medium saucepan over medium heat, melt butter. Add rice and stir for 1 minute. Add broth, salt, and pepper and bring to a boil. Reduce heat to medium-low and cook, covered, until rice is tender, about 20 minutes. Stir in Parmesan, pecans, and parsley. Fluff with a fork before serving.

2 tablespoons butter

1 cup long-grain white rice

2¼ cups chicken broth

¼ teaspoon salt

Freshly ground pepper to taste

¼ cup freshly grated Parmesan cheese

⅓ cup chopped pecans

3 tablespoons chopped fresh parsley

LEMON RICE WITH PINE NUTS

Serves 4

Rice is a gracious accompaniment to many main dishes because it doesn't overpower the flavor of other foods. This refreshing lemon-scented dish was created as a side to go with Grilled Salmon Fillets with Fresh Herb Coating (page 288), but serve it with any seafood dish.

In a medium saucepan over high heat, bring broth to a boil. Add rice, zest, green onions, salt, pepper, lemon juice, and capers. Reduce heat to medium-low and simmer, covered, until rice is tender and liquid is absorbed, about 20 minutes.

When rice is done, add pine nuts, parsley, and butter. Cover and let stand 5 minutes. Fluff with a fork before serving.

2¼ cups chicken broth

1 cup long-grain white rice

2 teaspoons grated lemon zest

¼ cup chopped green onions, including some tender green tops

½ teaspoon salt

Freshly ground pepper to taste

Juice of 1 lemon

1 tablespoon capers, drained

2 tablespoons pine nuts, toasted (see Note, page 206)

3 tablespoons chopped fresh parsley

1 tablespoon butter

ONION RICE

Serves 4

Sautéed onions added to rice makes a perfect side dish for beef. Serve with Broiled Steak with Herb Butter (page 91).

In a medium saucepan over medium-high heat, combine rice, broth, and salt and bring to a boil. Reduce heat to low and cook, covered, until rice is tender and liquid is absorbed, about 20 minutes. Remove from heat.

In a small skillet over medium heat, melt butter. Add onion and sauté until tender, about 5 minutes. Stir into rice. Add parsley and fluff with a fork before serving.

1   cup long-grain white rice
2¼ cups chicken, beef, or vegetable broth
¼   teaspoon salt
2   tablespoons butter
½   cup chopped yellow onion
¼   cup chopped fresh parsley

PASTA, GRAIN, AND LEGUME SIDE DISHES

FRIED RICE

Serves 4 to 6

My husband, Reed, does not like rice unless it includes other tasty ingredients. This is one of his favorites. Serve this complementary side dish with Asian food. Leftover pork can be added to make it a main course.

In a large skillet over medium heat, warm 1 tablespoon oil. Add onion, celery, and bell pepper and sauté until tender-crisp, about 5 minutes. Push the vegetables to the sides of the skillet and increase heat to medium-high. Add remaining ½ tablespoon oil to the middle of the skillet. When hot, add eggs in the middle of the skillet and scramble fast until dry. Stir together vegetables and eggs in the pan. Stir in rice and ⅓ cup soy sauce and mix well. Reduce heat to medium and cook several minutes longer until heated through, stirring occasionally. Pass extra soy sauce.

1½ tablespoons vegetable oil

½ cup chopped yellow onion

½ cup chopped celery

1 cup chopped green bell pepper

2 large eggs, lightly beaten

1 cup long-grain white rice, cooked according to package directions (3 cups cooked)

⅓ cup soy sauce, plus extra for serving

DOUBLE CORN POLENTA
Serves 6

Instead of rice, potatoes, or other starch dishes, try corn-meal polenta for a down-home side dish. Polenta is nourishing and tasty and goes well with a variety of main-course dishes. A staple of northern Italy, it may be baked, fried, or just served as a soft, bland mush. You can use the coarse grind of cornmeal labeled "polenta" if you wish, but I use regular cornmeal for equally savory results, as it cooks more quickly. In this dish, cheese, corn, and chilies are added, making it a substantial and exciting accompaniment to Mexican food when topped with salsa and sour cream.

Preheat oven to 350°F. In a bowl, combine melted butter, eggs, cheese, corn, cornmeal, 1 cup sour cream, sugar, salt, and chiles and mix well. Place in a lightly sprayed or oiled 7 ½-by-11¾-inch glass baking dish.

Bake, uncovered, until firm, about 40 minutes. Sprinkle with Parmesan cheese and bake 5 minutes longer. Serve with salsa and additional sour cream.

¼ cup (½ stick) butter, melted

2 large eggs, beaten

1 cup grated Cheddar cheese

1 package (10 ounces) frozen corn, thawed and well drained

½ cup yellow cornmeal

1 cup sour cream, plus more for serving

1 tablespoon sugar

1 teaspoon salt

1 can (4 ounces) chopped green chiles, drained

¼ cup freshly grated Parmesan cheese

Fresh Tomato Salsa (page 71) or good-quality purchased tomato salsa for serving

BLACK BEAN AND CORN CASSEROLE

Serves 6

You can rely on your favorite Mexican ingredients and flavors in this layered vegetarian casserole. Serve with a complementary Orange, Cucumber, and Red Onion Salad with Lime-Cumin Dressing (page 54).

Preheat oven to 350°F. In a large skillet over medium heat, warm oil. Add onion, bell pepper, and garlic and sauté until tender, about 5 minutes. Add tomato sauce, salsa, oregano, chili powder, cumin, salt, and pepper. Stir in beans and corn.

In a lightly sprayed or oiled 9-by-13-inch glass baking dish, spread one-third of the bean mixture evenly over the bottom of the dish. Lay 4 tortillas on top slightly overlapping. Add another one-third of the bean mixture and half of the cheese. Add 4 more tortillas, remaining bean mixture, and top with remaining cheese. Cover with aluminum foil and bake for 30 minutes. Uncover and bake until bubbly, about 10 minutes longer. Let stand for 10 minutes before serving. Cut into squares to serve. Pass sour cream in a bowl.

2	teaspoons vegetable oil
1	cup chopped yellow onion
½	cup chopped red or green bell pepper
2	garlic cloves, minced
1	can (8 ounces) tomato sauce
½	cup Fresh Tomato Salsa (page 71) or good-quality purchased tomato salsa
½	teaspoon dried oregano
½	teaspoon chili powder
¼	teaspoon ground cumin
¼	teaspoon salt
	Freshly ground pepper to taste
2	cans (15 ounces each) black beans, drained and rinsed
1	cup corn, fresh or frozen
8	corn tortillas
4	cups grated Cheddar cheese
	Sour cream for serving

FOUR-BEAN BAKE

Serves 10 to 12

Beans are healthful, full of flavor, and nearly fat free. They are high in fiber, low in calories, and a good source of minerals. Here four kinds of beans are combined with a chile sauce and baked in the oven. This is a perfect side dish for a picnic supper with hamburgers or hot dogs.

Preheat oven to 350ºF. Combine all ingredients in a lightly sprayed or oiled 3-quart casserole and mix well. Bake, covered, until bubbly, about 1 hour and 15 minutes, stirring occasionally. Discard bay leaf before serving. If beans become dry, add more ketchup.

1	large yellow onion, chopped
1	can (8 ounces) tomato sauce
1	tablespoon prepared mustard
½	cup chili sauce or ketchup
2	tablespoons cider vinegar
2	tablespoons molasses
1	bay leaf
¼	teaspoon dried thyme
½	teaspoon chili powder
½	teaspoon salt
	Freshly ground pepper to taste
1	can (15 ounces) red kidney beans, drained and rinsed
1	can (15 ounces) black beans, drained and rinsed
1	can (15 ounces) cannellini (white kidney) beans, drained and rinsed
1	can (15 ounces) garbanzo beans, drained and rinsed
1	can (4 ounces) chopped green chiles, drained

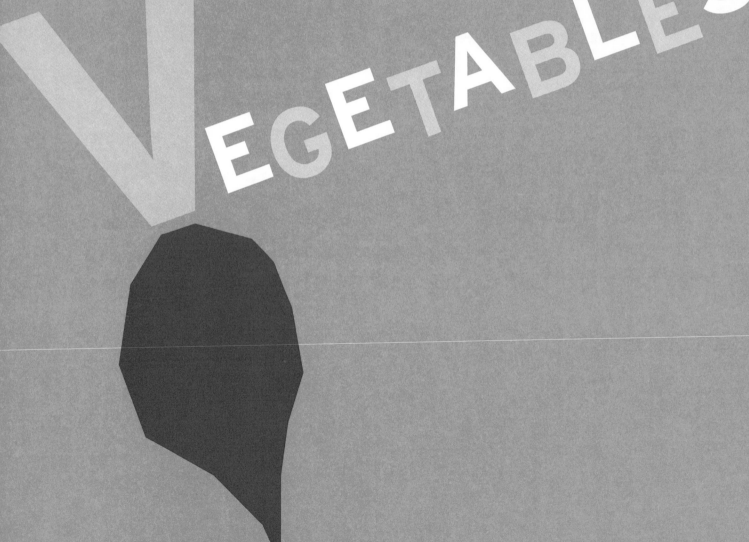

VEGETABLES

CHAPTER 11

EXCITING NEW WAYS WITH VEGETABLES

Vegetables are generally served as a side dish to round out the meal, or for the vegetarian and other vegetable lovers, they may serve as the main course. Vegetables add color, texture, and contrast and provide essential vitamins, minerals, and fiber.

Vegetables must be cooked properly; if overcooked, they lose valuable nutrients, flavor, color, and become soggy and boring. Although cooking times are listed in these recipes, this will vary depending on the size and freshness of vegetables and on your personal preference. Check for doneness frequently.

Don't be satisfied with the same old ordinary vegetables. Try some of these innovative new ideas, such as Asparagus with Cashew Butter (page 213); Green Beans with Tomatoes, Garlic, and Feta Cheese (page 207); Italian Sautéed Peppers (page 216); Potato Wedges (page 220); and many more.

BROCCOLI WITH HERB BUTTER

Serves 6

Easy to cook, healthful, and colorful, fresh broccoli is available year-round. Here, it is simply seasoned with butter and herbs. To retain its appealing emerald green color, do not overcook.

In a large saucepan over medium heat, cook broccoli in lightly salted, gently boiling water to cover, and cook until tender-crisp, 6 to 7 minutes. Drain well. Add butter and seasonings and toss with broccoli until butter is melted and broccoli is heated through, about 1 minute.

2   pounds broccoli, tough stalks trimmed, cut into serving pieces
¼   cup (½ stick) butter
½   teaspoon dried basil
½   teaspoon dried marjoram
½   teaspoon dried thyme
½   teaspoon salt
     Freshly ground pepper to taste

BROCCOLI WITH MUSTARD BUTTER
Serves 6

In the winter when garden-fresh vegetables are not always available, perk up this broccoli side dish with a savory topping.

In a large saucepan over medium heat, cook broccoli in lightly salted, gently boiling water to cover until tender-crisp, 6 to 7 minutes. Drain well.

In a small pan over medium heat, melt butter with mustard, lemon juice, salt, and pepper (or microwave 30 seconds in a cup) and toss with drained broccoli. Serve immediately.

2	pounds broccoli, tough stalks trimmed, cut into serving pieces
¼	cup (½ stick) butter
1	tablespoon Dijon mustard
2	teaspoons fresh lemon juice
¼	teaspoon salt
	Freshly ground pepper to taste

LEMONY GREEN BEANS WITH TOASTED PINE NUTS

Serves 4

Pine nuts add extra flavor and crunch to these lemony green beans. Pine nuts are the seeds of pine cones from several varieties of pine trees. They can be purchased in bulk or in packages. Because of their high fat content, store them in a plastic bag in the refrigerator, or freeze for up to 6 months. This vegetable dish goes well with Grilled Salmon Steaks with Dill Sauce (page 287).

In a medium saucepan over medium heat, cook beans in lightly salted, gently boiling water to cover until tender-crisp, 6 to 7 minutes. Drain and add butter, lemon juice, and salt and pepper. Add pine nuts and mix well. Serve immediately.

1   pound green beans, trimmed

1   tablespoon butter

1   tablespoon fresh lemon juice

    Salt and freshly ground pepper to taste

1½ tablespoons pine nuts, toasted (see Note)

NOTE: To toast pine nuts, place in a small nonstick skillet over medium heat and stir constantly until lightly browned, 2 to 3 minutes. Watch carefully to prevent burning and transfer immediately to a plate to cool; the nuts will continue to cook while cooling.

GREEN BEANS WITH TOMATOES, GARLIC, AND FETA CHEESE

Serves 4

This combination of crisp green beans and a garlicky tomato sauce topped with feta cheese makes a colorful accompaniment to many dishes, especially Chicken Bobsie (page 127).

In a medium saucepan over medium heat, cook beans in lightly salted, gently boiling water to cover until tender-crisp, 6 to 7 minutes. Drain under cold water and set aside.

In a medium skillet over medium heat, melt butter with oil. Add tomatoes, garlic, and ¼ cup parsley. Sauté until vegetables are tender, about 2 minutes. Add beans, salt, and pepper and simmer a few minutes to reheat and blend flavors. Serve in a bowl sprinkled with remaining parsley and feta cheese.

1 pound fresh green beans, trimmed
2 tablespoons butter
1 tablespoon vegetable oil
2 plum (Roma) tomatoes, coarsely chopped
2 large garlic cloves, minced
¼ cup chopped fresh parsley, plus 2 tablespoons
¼ teaspoon salt
Freshly ground pepper to taste
¼ cup crumbled feta cheese

STEAMED HERBED CARROTS AND BROCCOLI

Serves 4 to 6

For an easy winter vegetable dish, steamed carrots and broccoli are tossed with a light mixture of lemon juice, butter, and herbs. Herbes de Provence is an assortment of dried herbs commonly used in France and can be purchased at most supermarkets. It is also used as a seasoning for other vegetables and poultry.

In a saucepan fitted with a steamer basket over medium-high heat, bring 1 inch of water to a boil. Add carrots, cover, and steam for 5 minutes. Add broccoli and steam until both vegetables are tender, about 6 minutes longer. Remove steamer basket, drain, and return vegetables to the pan. Add butter, lemon juice, salt, and herbes de Provence and toss to coat.

2   carrots, cut into 2-inch pieces and then sliced into narrow strips
3   cups broccoli florets
2   tablespoons butter
1   tablespoon fresh lemon juice
½   teaspoon salt
½   teaspoon herbes de Provence

CAULIFLOWER TOPPED WITH CHEESE

Serves 6

Cauliflower is a member of the cruciferous family and a relative of cabbage, Brussels sprouts, and broccoli. It is composed of tiny florets on clusters of stalks. It is good raw for snacking or cooked and is a good source of vitamin C and iron. Simply prepared, this recipe requires little time and few ingredients.

Preheat broiler. In a medium saucepan over medium heat, bring just enough water to cover cauliflower to a boil. Add cauliflower, cover, and cook until tender, 6 to 7 minutes. Drain and toss with butter and salt and pepper. Place in an ovenproof serving dish and sprinkle with cheese. Broil until cheese melts, about 1 minute. Serve immediately.

1   head cauliflower, trimmed and cut into serving pieces
2   tablespoons butter
    Salt and freshly ground pepper to taste
1   cup grated Cheddar cheese

LEMON CAULIFLOWER

Serves 4

Cooking cauliflower with lemon slices helps retain its snowy white color and adds a sharp, bright flavor. Serve with Lamb Chops with Crumb Topping (page 110).

In a medium saucepan over medium heat, bring just enough water to cover cauliflower to a boil. Add cauliflower and lemon slices, cover, and cook until tender, 5 to 6 minutes. Drain and remove lemon slices. Toss with butter, salt, pepper, and parsley and serve immediately.

5   cups cauliflower florets
3   lemon slices
2   tablespoons butter
½   teaspoon salt
    Freshly ground pepper to taste
2   tablespoons chopped fresh parsley

STEAMED BABY CARROTS

Serves 4

Ready-to-eat baby carrots in a bag are convenient and do not require any prepping. Here, butter, honey, and herbs are added for an easy vegetable side dish. Serve with Harvest Pork Roast (page 104).

In a saucepan fitted with a steamer basket over medium-high heat, bring 1 inch of water to a gentle boil. Add carrots, cover, and steam until tender, about 15 minutes. Remove steamer basket, drain, and return carrots to the pan. Add butter, honey, salt and pepper, and herbs and mix well. Serve immediately.

4   cups baby carrots, rinsed and drained
2   tablespoons butter
2   tablespoons honey
    Salt and freshly ground pepper to taste
½   teaspoon herbs de Provence

ASPARAGUS WITH CREAMY LEMON SAUCE OR ROASTED RED BELL PEPPER AIOLI

Serves 4

Fresh asparagus is so good it can be served with just butter, salt, and pepper, or enhanced with one of these easy toppings for a company supper.

In a large skillet over medium heat, cook asparagus in gently boiling, lightly salted water to cover until tender-crisp, 5 to 6 minutes. Drain well and toss with butter and salt and pepper. Serve plain or with the sauce of your choice on the side.

1   pound asparagus, tough ends snapped off
1   tablespoon butter
    Salt and freshly ground pepper to taste

CHOICE OF SAUCES
Creamy Lemon Sauce (recipe follows)
Roasted Red Bell Pepper Aioli (page 165)

CREAMY LEMON SAUCE

In a small bowl, mix together all ingredients until smooth. Serve at room temperature.

Makes about ½ cup

¼   cup mayonnaise
¼   cup plain nonfat yogurt
2   tablespoons fresh lemon juice
2   drops Tabasco sauce
¼   teaspoon salt

ASPARAGUS WITH CASHEW BUTTER

Serves 4 to 6

For a springtime treat, serve tender-crisp asparagus topped with sautéed cashews along with Pork Chops with Sour Cream–Dill Sauce (page 102).

In a large skillet over medium heat, cook asparagus in gently boiling, lightly salted water to cover until tender-crisp, 5 to 6 minutes. Drain and transfer to a plate. In the same skillet, melt butter. Stir in cashews and sauté until golden, about 2 minutes. Add lemon juice, salt, and pepper. Return asparagus to skillet and stir until heated through, about 1 minute. Serve immediately.

1¼	pounds asparagus, tough ends snapped off
3	tablespoons butter
¼	cup coarsely chopped cashews
2	teaspoons fresh lemon juice
¼	teaspoon salt
	Freshly ground pepper to taste

CORN ON THE COB WITH TWO BUTTERS

Serves 4

Fresh corn is best when eaten as soon as possible after picking. Store in the refrigerator and do not husk until ready to cook. Today's corn is so tender it only needs to be warmed through. For variety, try one of the compound butters included here.

Bring a large pot of water over high heat to a boil. Add corn and return to a boil. Boil for 4 minutes. Do not add salt (it toughens the corn). Drain and serve immediately with one of the following spreads.

4 ears sweet corn, husks and silks removed
Herb Butter (recipe follows)
Lime Butter (recipe on facing page)

HERB BUTTER

This butter is delicious on all vegetables and on warmed French bread.
Use your favorite herbs.

Wash and dry herbs. Combine all ingredients in a food processor and process to blend well, scraping down sides of bowl with a spatula as needed. Transfer to a small bowl, cover, and refrigerate. Serve at room temperature.

Makes about ½ cup

1 teaspoon snipped fresh thyme or ½ teaspoon dried thyme
1 teaspoon snipped fresh oregano or ½ teaspoon dried oregano
4 fresh basil leaves, torn into pieces, or ½ teaspoon dried basil
4 fresh chive stalks, coarsely chopped
3 sprigs fresh parsley
½ cup (1 stick) butter, at room temperature, cut into tablespoons

LIME BUTTER

Combine all ingredients in a medium microwave-safe bowl. Heat in microwave oven on high until butter is melted, about 30 seconds. Remove and stir until blended. Cover and refrigerate until firm. Serve at room temperature.

Makes about ½ cup

½   cup (1 stick) butter, at room temperature
2   tablespoons fresh lime juice
1   teaspoon grated lime zest
¼   teaspoon dry mustard
⅛   teaspoon Tabasco sauce

ITALIAN SAUTÉED PEPPERS

Serves 4 to 6

Bell peppers are sweet, mild flavored, and do not have the heat of other peppers. This platter of sautéed peppers in a variety of colors makes an attractive accompaniment to grilled meats.

In a large skillet over medium heat, melt butter with 1 tablespoon oil. Add bell peppers, onion, garlic, basil, oregano, salt, and pepper and sauté until bell peppers are tender, 7 to 8 minutes. Add remaining ½ tablespoon oil if needed. Add wine and cook several minutes. Transfer to a platter and garnish with basil leaves.

1   tablespoon butter

1   to 1½ tablespoons vegetable oil

3   bell peppers (1 red, 1 green, and 1 yellow), seeded and cut into ½-inch-wide strips

1   yellow onion, sliced and separated into rings

2   garlic cloves, minced

1   tablespoon chopped fresh basil or ½ teaspoon dried basil

½   teaspoon dried oregano

½   teaspoon salt
    Freshly ground pepper to taste

¼   cup dry white wine
    Fresh basil leaves for garnish

SMASHED POTATOES WITH BLUE CHEESE AND CHIVES

Serves 4

If cooked potatoes are mashed until smooth, they are called mashed potatoes. If they are slightly mashed and still chunky (usually new potatoes), they are called smashed. Here these tender new potatoes are combined with sour cream and blue cheese for a different taste.

In a medium saucepan over medium-high heat, bring just enough water to cover potatoes to a boil. Add potatoes, cover, and cook until tender, about 20 minutes. Drain well. With a potato masher, smash potatoes until chunky. Stir in salt, pepper, sour cream, blue cheese, and chives.

4   medium unpeeled new red potatoes (about 1½ pounds), scrubbed and quartered

½   teaspoon salt
     Freshly ground pepper to taste

½   cup sour cream

½   cup crumbled blue cheese

2   tablespoons chopped fresh chives

CHEESY POTATOES

Serves 8 to 10

This is a convenient side dish suitable for making ahead. If preferred, light sour cream and 2 percent milk can be used to reduce calories; the potatoes will be just as good. This dish is a great accompaniment with meats.

In a large saucepan over medium-high heat, bring just enough water to cover potatoes to a boil. Add potatoes, cover, and cook until tender, about 15 minutes. Drain, let cool, and cut into ¼ inch slices.

Preheat oven to 350°F. Place potatoes in a lightly sprayed or oiled 4-quart casserole. Add remaining ingredients, reserving 1 cup cheese, and mix well. Sprinkle remaining cheese on top. Bake, uncovered, until bubbly, about 35 minutes.

10   unpeeled new potatoes (about 3 pounds), scrubbed and halved

½   cup chopped green onions, including some tender green tops

2   cups sour cream

¼   cup chopped fresh parsley

3   cups grated Cheddar cheese

½   cup whole milk

1   teaspoon salt

Freshly ground pepper to taste

TWICE-BAKED POTATOES

Serves 4

One of my grandsons always requests these potatoes when he comes to supper. This is a quick and easy way to make twice-baked potatoes without the steps of mashing the pulp and refilling the shells.

4	medium unpeeled russet potatoes (about 2 pounds), scrubbed
	Salt and freshly ground pepper to taste
4	teaspoons butter
¼	cup sour cream
¼	cup grated Cheddar cheese

Preheat oven to 350°F. Bake potatoes until softened, about 1 hour. Remove from oven and cut a slit across the top. Squeeze the potato to open slightly. To each potato, add salt and pepper, 1 teaspoon butter, 1 tablespoon sour cream, and 1 tablespoon cheese and blend thoroughly with a fork. Return to the oven and bake until cheese is melted, about 10 minutes longer.

VARIATION: Substitute cottage cheese for sour cream.

POTATO WEDGES

Serves 4

These potato wedges are baked in the oven instead of deep-fat fried to reduce the calories. Served with ketchup for dipping, they taste like French fries. They are a natural paired with Grilled Cabin Burgers (page 271).

Preheat oven to 425°F. In a large shallow bowl, combine potatoes, olive oil, rosemary, salt, and pepper and toss to coat. Arrange on a baking sheet in a single layer. Bake, uncovered, until golden brown and crisp, 25 to 30 minutes. Serve immediately with ketchup on the side.

4 medium russet potatoes (about 1½ pounds), peeled and cut lengthwise into 8 wedges
1 tablespoon olive oil
½ teaspoon dried rosemary (optional)
½ teaspoon coarse salt
¼ teaspoon freshly ground pepper
   Ketchup for dipping

BAKED POPPY SEED ONIONS
Serves 4

Onion slices and mild shallots are baked in a creamy sauce accented with poppy seeds. This is a great side dish to serve with a beef roast for a winter supper.

Preheat oven to 350°F. Place onion rings, shallots, and green onions in a lightly sprayed or oiled 2-quart casserole. Stir in salt, pepper, and poppy seeds. In a medium bowl, blend cream cheese with milk. Pour over onions and mix well. Cover and bake until onions are tender and creamy, about 1 hour.

2   large yellow onions (about 1½ pounds), sliced and rings separated (about 4 cups)

2   shallots, chopped

4   green onions, including some tender green tops, sliced

¼   teaspoon salt

¼   teaspoon freshly ground pepper

2   tablespoons poppy seeds

3   ounces cream cheese, at room temperature

½   cup whole milk

SPINACH WITH BACON AND EGG TOPPING

This is a family-favorite way to cook spinach. It looks like a lot when it goes into the saucepan, but remember, spinach has a way of shrinking fast. Serve with Grilled Salmon Steaks with Dill Sauce (page 287).

In a large saucepan over medium heat, cook spinach in 2 tablespoons water, tossing with 2 forks several times until wilted, about 5 minutes. Drain well and season with butter and salt and pepper and mix well. Transfer to a bowl and top with egg and bacon.

2   bags (12 ounces each) baby spinach, stems removed if desired

3   tablespoons butter
    Salt and freshly ground pepper to taste

1   or 2 hard-cooked large eggs, peeled and chopped

3   bacon strips, cooked until crisp, drained, and crumbled

SAUTÉED SPINACH, GARLIC, AND MUSHROOMS

Serves 4 to 6

In this side dish, sautéed mushrooms and garlic are tossed with fresh spinach until the spinach is wilted and ready to eat. The three flavors here make a great combination of vegetables.

In a large saucepan over medium heat, melt butter with olive oil. Add mushrooms and garlic and sauté until tender, about 5 minutes. Add spinach and toss with 2 forks until wilted, about 5 minutes. Season with salt and pepper and mix well. Serve immediately.

1   tablespoon butter

1   tablespoon olive oil

6   ounces mushrooms, sliced

2   large garlic cloves, minced

2   bags (12 ounces each) spinach, stems removed, if desired

½   teaspoon salt

Freshly ground pepper to taste

SWEET ACORN SQUASH

Serves 4

Maple syrup mixed with nuts and butter makes a sweet, crunchy filling for squash in this fall vegetable side dish. Bake along with Lamb and Turkey Loaf (page 111) for an easy oven supper.

Preheat oven to 350°F. Place squash, cut sides up, on a baking sheet. Add 1 teaspoon each butter, syrup, walnuts, and raisins (if using) to each squash half. Bake until tender, about 1 hour.

2   acorn squash, halved and seeded
4   teaspoons butter
4   teaspoons pure maple syrup or honey
4   teaspoons chopped walnuts
4   teaspoons raisins (optional)

ZUCCHINI BAKE

Serves 4 to 6

There is never a shortage of zucchini in the late summer and fall to make this easy vegetable casserole.

Preheat oven to 350°F. In a lightly sprayed or oiled 2-quart casserole, layer half of the zucchini. Add tomato and onion slices on top. Season with dill and salt and pepper. Layer remaining zucchini on top. Cover and bake for 40 minutes. Pour off any excess liquid that may have accumulated. Sprinkle with cheeses and bake, uncovered, until vegetables are tender and cheese is melted, about 5 minutes longer.

2   large zucchini, unpeeled, cut into 3/8-inch slices
1   large tomato, sliced
1/2 yellow onion, sliced
1/4 teaspoon dried dill
    Salt and freshly ground pepper to taste
3/4 cup grated Cheddar cheese
1   tablespoon grated Parmesan cheese

ZUCCHINI BOATS

Serves 4

Zucchini is so versatile it can be prepared many ways. Here it is briefly parboiled, then halved and baked in the oven with a flavorful topping

Preheat oven to 350°F. In a medium saucepan over high heat, parboil zucchini in boiling water for 4 minutes. Drain under cold water. Cut zucchini halves in half lengthwise and place in a lightly sprayed or oiled 8-by-8-inch glass baking dish. Brush with olive oil. Season with oregano and salt and pepper. Sprinkle with bread crumbs and Parmesan. Bake until zucchini is tender, about 10 minutes.

2   zucchini, unpeeled, halved crosswise
     Olive oil for brushing
¼   teaspoon dried oregano
     Salt and freshly ground pepper to taste
¼   cup fine dried bread crumbs
¼   cup freshly grated Parmesan cheese

GARLIC ROASTED VEGETABLES

Serves 4 to 6

This colorful dish of mixed vegetables makes a complementary side dish for grilled meats. Roasting vegetables intensifies their natural flavor and helps retain vitamins and minerals. You may vary the vegetables you use according to the season and your preference.

Preheat oven to 400°F. In a large bowl, combine all ingredients and toss well to coat. In a lightly sprayed or oiled 9-by-13-inch glass baking dish, spread vegetables in a single layer. Roast until vegetables are tender-crisp, 35 to 40 minutes, stirring once.

1   green bell pepper, seeded and cut into 1½-inch strips

1   red bell pepper, seeded and cut into 1½-inch strips

2   zucchini, unpeeled, cut into ¾-inch pieces

1   red onion, sliced

10 whole garlic cloves, peeled

1   tablespoon chopped fresh basil leaves or ¾ teaspoon dried basil

1   tablespoon chopped fresh rosemary or ½ teaspoon dried rosemary

2½ tablespoons vegetable oil

1   tablespoon balsamic vinegar

¾   teaspoon salt

    Freshly ground pepper to taste

SUMMER VEGETABLE SAUTÉ

Serves 6

If you don't grow your own vegetables, visit the farmers' market or road-side produce stand and enjoy the fresh flavor of garden vegetables in this easy skillet dish.

In a large skillet over medium heat, melt butter with oil. Add onion, garlic, bell pepper, mushrooms, and zucchini and sauté for 5 minutes. Add corn, salt, pepper, and basil and sauté until vegetables are tender, about 5 minutes longer. Serve immediately.

2   tablespoons butter

1   tablespoon vegetable oil

½   cup chopped yellow onion

1   garlic clove, chopped

1   red bell pepper, seeded and cut into 1-inch pieces

8   ounces mushrooms, quartered

2   zucchini, unpeeled, cut into ½-inch slices

1½   cups fresh corn kernels (cut from 2 or 3 ears of corn)

½   teaspoon salt

     Freshly ground pepper to taste

1   tablespoon chopped fresh basil

WINTER VEGETABLE SAUTÉ

Serves 4

This eye-catching combination of lightly sautéed vegetables will add variety to your winter menu.

In a large skillet over medium heat, warm oil. Add onion, garlic, bell pepper, broccoli, and carrot and sauté for 4 minutes. Add mushrooms and sauté for 5 minutes longer. Stir in wine, basil, salt, and pepper. Cover and simmer until vegetables are tender, about 5 minutes longer.

2 tablespoons vegetable oil
½ cup chopped yellow onion
1 garlic clove, minced
½ cup chopped red bell pepper
3 cups broccoli florets
1 carrot, thinly sliced
6 mushrooms, quartered
2 tablespoons dry white wine
½ teaspoon dried basil
¼ teaspoon salt
Freshly ground pepper to taste

CHAPTER 12

POPULAR AND INVENTIVE NEW COMBINATIONS

Suppertime can be a lot of fun for the whole family when you serve pizza. Pizzas are easy to make and can be put together in less time than a delivery from the pizza parlor. Very little equipment is needed and prepared crusts and sauces have revolutionized pizza making for the home cook. On the next page is a summary of the basics for running your own pizza kitchen.

PIZZA BASICS

EQUIPMENT
You will need a pizza pan or baking sheet, pizza-cutting wheel or sharp knife, and a pizza stone if making homemade crusts.

INGREDIENTS
CRUSTS: There are several options for crusts. The easiest is to buy a prepared crust, such as prebaked Boboli or focaccia. Also available are pizza crust mixes, frozen pizza crust dough, and frozen bread dough, or you can make your own crust from scratch. It is easy to make homemade crust in the food processor.

SAUCES: A variety of sauces can be used, including homemade sauces, purchased pizza sauce, tomato sauce, tomato purée, tomato paste, marinara sauce, salsa and pesto.

TOPPINGS: You can be as creative as you like with combinations of your choice, but be aware, it is often a mistake to be tempted to add too many ingredients. A maximum of three or four toppings is recommended in addition to the sauce and cheese. Pizzas are also a tasty way to use up leftovers like vegetables, bits of meat, and seafood.

ASSEMBLING
Spread the sauce on the crust, add the toppings, and bake immediately.

BAKING
Bake pizza at 450ºF in the middle of the oven until the crust is crisp and the sauce and cheese are bubbly, about 10 minutes. Transfer to a cutting board and, using a pizza-cutting wheel or sharp knife, slice into 8 wedges. Serve immediately.

FOOD-PROCESSOR PIZZA DOUGH
Makes 2 crusts

If you want your own crust, let the food processor do the kneading for you and reduce preparation time. See the facing page for other pizza crust options.

In a 2-cup measuring cup, stir together water, yeast, and sugar until dissolved. Set aside.

In food processor, place flour and salt and blend. Stir 2 tablespoons oil into the yeast mixture. With the motor running, slowly pour the yeast mixture through the feed tube. Allow the dough to go around the bowl until the dough clings together, about 20 to 30 times. Turn out onto a floured board and knead until dough is smooth and elastic, 5 or 6 times. Cut dough into 2 equal pieces. Form each piece into a round disk and let rest 10 minutes. With a floured rolling pin, roll out the disks into 12-inch circles. Brush pizza pan with oil and lightly sprinkle with cornmeal. Transfer crust to the pan, pressing the dough with your fingers to the edge of the pan. Add toppings and proceed as directed in the recipe.

1   cup warm water (105° to 115°F)
1   package (¼ ounce) rapid fire yeast
1   teaspoon sugar
3   cups all-purpose flour, plus more as needed
1   teaspoon salt
2   tablespoons vegetable oil, plus additional oil for brushing on pizza pan
    Cornmeal for sprinkling on pizza pan

HOMEMADE PIZZA SAUCE

Homemade pizza sauce is easy to make.

In a small saucepan over high heat, combine all ingredients. Bring to a boil, reduce heat, and simmer, uncovered, until flavors are blended, about 10 minutes.

Makes about 1¼ cups (enough for 2 pizzas)

1   can (10¾ ounces) tomato purée
¼   teaspoon dried marjoram
¼   teaspoon dried basil
¼   teaspoon oregano
¼   teaspoon onion powder
¼   teaspoon salt
     Freshly ground pepper to taste
1   tablespoon finely chopped parsley
1   garlic clove, minced

FAVORITE PEPPERONI-MUSHROOM PIZZA

Serves 4

This is one of the most popular pizzas with all ages. Serve with cold beer, iced tea, or soda.

Preheat oven to 450°F. Place crust on a pizza pan or baking sheet. Spread crust with sauce to ½ inch from the edge. Sprinkle with 1 cup of the cheese. Add the mushrooms. Arrange pepperoni slices in a circle on top, slightly overlapping. Sprinkle with the remaining cheese. Bake until crust is crisp and topping is bubbly, about 10 minutes. Transfer to a cutting board and, using a pizza-cutting wheel or sharp knife, slice into 8 wedges. Serve immediately.

1   12-inch pizza crust, homemade (page 233) or purchased

½   cup pizza sauce, homemade (page 233) or purchased

1½ cups grated mozzarella cheese

4   ounces mushrooms, sliced

1   can (2¼ ounces) sliced olives, drained

1   package (3 ounces) sliced pepperoni

CANADIAN BACON AND PINEAPPLE PIZZA

Serves 4

The pineapple adds a sweet flavor that contrasts nicely with the bacon in this popular pizza. If hosting a pizza party, include this one for variety.

Preheat oven to 450°F. Place crust on a pizza pan or baking sheet. Spread crust with sauce to ½ inch from the edge. Top with bacon, pineapple, and green onions. Sprinkle with cheeses. Bake until crust is crisp and topping is bubbly, about 10 minutes. Transfer to a cutting board and, using a pizza-cutting wheel or sharp knife, slice into 8 wedges. Serve immediately.

1   12-inch pizza crust, homemade (page 233) or purchased

½   cup pizza sauce, homemade (page 233) or purchased

6   ounces sliced Canadian bacon

1   can (8 ounces) pineapple chunks, drained

¼   cup sliced green onions, including some tender green tops

½   cup grated Cheddar cheese

½   cup grated Monterey Jack cheese

HOT LIPS PIZZA

Serves 4

Enjoy the popular "South of the Border" ingredients of beef, salsa, and chiles in this fun and flavorful combination. Sip a glass of cool sangria with this pizza.

Preheat oven to 450°F. In a large skillet over medium heat, combine beef, onion, and garlic and sauté, breaking up meat with a spoon, until meat is browned and vegetables are tender, about 5 minutes, adding a little oil if needed. Season with salt and pepper. Place crust on a pizza pan or baking sheet. Spread crust with salsa to ½ inch from the edge. Sprinkle with 1 cup cheese. Add meat mixture and remaining cheese. Scatter olives over the top. Bake until crust is crisp and topping is bubbly, about 10 minutes. Transfer to a cutting board and, using a pizza-cutting wheel or sharp knife, slice into 8 wedges. Garnish with avocado slices.

½   pound ground beef

½   cup chopped yellow onion

2   garlic cloves, minced
    Vegetable oil, as needed

½   teaspoon salt
    Freshly ground pepper to taste

1   12-inch pizza crust, homemade (page 233) or purchased

¾   cup Fresh Tomato Salsa (page 71) or good-quality purchased tomato salsa

2   cups grated pepper Jack cheese

1   cup sliced black olives

1   avocado, peeled, pitted, and sliced

CHICKEN, MUSHROOM, AND AVOCADO PIZZA

Serves 4

This pizza makes good use of leftover chicken combined with other favorite ingredients for a delicious pizza. Turkey can also be used.

Preheat oven to 450°F. Place crust on a pizza pan or baking sheet. Spread crust with sauce to ½ inch from the edge. Sprinkle with 1 cup cheese. Add mushrooms, chicken, and avocado. Sprinkle with salt and remaining cheese. Bake until crust is crisp and topping is bubbly, about 10 minutes. Transfer to a cutting board and, using a pizza-cutting wheel or sharp knife, slice into 8 wedges. Serve immediately.

1	12-inch pizza crust, homemade (page 233) or purchased
½	cup pizza sauce, homemade (page 233) or purchased
2	cups grated Monterey Jack cheese
3	ounces mushrooms, sliced
1½	cups cubed cooked chicken breast (see Note, page 30)
1	avocado, peeled, pitted, and cut into bite-sized pieces
¼	teaspoon salt

CHICKEN, PESTO, AND TOMATO PIZZA

Serves 4

Pesto adds a distinctive flavor to this pizza. Bay shrimp can be used instead of chicken, or for variety, try it half chicken and half shrimp.

Preheat oven to 450°F. Place crust on a pizza pan or baking sheet. Spread crust with pesto to ½ inch from the edge. Sprinkle with 1 cup Jack cheese. Add chicken and sprinkle remaining Jack cheese over. Top with tomato slices and sprinkle with Parmesan. Bake until crust is crisp and topping is bubbly, about 10 minutes. Transfer to a cutting board and, using a pizza-cutting wheel or sharp knife, slice into 8 wedges. Serve immediately.

1   12-inch pizza crust, homemade (page 233) or purchased

½   cup Basil Pesto, homemade (page 190) or purchased

2   cups grated Monterey Jack cheese

2   cups cubed cooked chicken breast (see Note, page 30)

1   plum (Roma) tomato, thinly sliced

¼   cup freshly grated Parmesan cheese

GROWN-UP PIZZA

Serves 4

Smoked turkey breast and artichokes go into this pizza that will appeal to adults—but who knows, kids might like it, too.

Preheat oven to 450°F. Place crust on a pizza pan or baking sheet. Spread crust with sauce to within ½ inch from the edge. Sprinkle with 1 cup cheese. Add turkey, artichokes, mushrooms, and green onions. Sprinkle with remaining cheese. Bake until crust is crisp and topping is bubbly, about 10 minutes. Transfer to a cutting board and, using a pizza-cutting wheel or sharp knife, slice into 8 wedges. Serve immediately.

1   12-inch pizza crust, homemade (page 233) or purchased

½   cup pizza sauce, homemade (page 233) or purchased

2   cups grated mozzarella cheese, divided

½   pound smoked or plain roasted turkey breast, diced

1   jar (6 ounces) marinated quartered artichoke hearts, drained and chopped

4   ounces mushrooms, sliced

4   to 6 green onions, including some tender green tops, sliced

SMOKED ITALIAN SAUSAGE, CHEESE, AND TOMATO PIZZA

Serves 4

Smoked sausage and cheese make a quick topping for this pizza that can be made in minutes.

Preheat oven to 450°F. Place crust on a pizza pan or baking sheet. Spread crust with sauce to ½ inch from the edge. Sprinkle with 1 cup cheese. Add sausages, bell pepper, green onions, remaining cheese, and tomatoes. Bake until the crust is crisp and topping is bubbly, about 10 minutes. Transfer to a cutting board and, using a pizza-cutting wheel or sharp knife, slice into 8 wedges. Serve immediately.

1	12-inch pizza crust, homemade (page 233) or purchased
½	cup pizza sauce, homemade (page 233) or purchased
2	cups grated mozzarella cheese
2	smoked Italian sausages, thinly sliced
½	green bell pepper, thinly sliced
¼	cup sliced green onions, including some tender green tops
2	plum (Roma) tomatoes, thinly sliced

TASTER'S CHOICE PIZZA

Serves 4

When we had friends over for a tasting party, this pizza was voted one of the best.

Preheat oven to 450°F. In a medium skillet over medium heat, combine sausage, bell pepper, and onion and sauté, breaking up meat with a spoon, until meat is browned and vegetables are tender, about 5 minutes. Place crust on a pizza pan or baking sheet. Spread crust with sauce to ½ inch from the edge. Sprinkle with 1 cup cheese. Add sausage mixture. Arrange pepperoni slices on top. Sprinkle with remaining cheese. Bake until the crust is crisp and top is bubbly, about 10 minutes. Transfer to a cutting board and, using a pizza-cutting wheel or sharp knife, slice into 8 wedges. Serve immediately.

½   pound bulk pork sausage

¼   cup chopped green bell pepper

¼   cup chopped yellow onion

1   12-inch pizza crust, homemade (page 233) or purchased

½   cup pizza sauce, homemade (page 233) or purchased

1½ cups grated Cheddar cheese

1   package (3 ounces) sliced pepperoni

MEXICAN BLACK BEAN AND CORN PIZZA

Serves 4

Combine a cool contrast by serving this colorful pizza of zesty Mexican flavors with Orange, Cucumber, and Red Onion Salad with Lime-Cumin Dressing (page 54).

Preheat oven to 450°F. Place crust on a pizza pan or baking sheet. Spread crust with salsa to ½ inch from the edge. Sprinkle with 1 cup cheese. Add beans, cilantro, corn, bell pepper, and olives. Sprinkle with remaining cheese. Bake until crust is crisp and topping is bubbly, about 10 minutes. Transfer to a cutting board and, using a pizza-cutting wheel or sharp knife, slice into 8 wedges.

1   12-inch pizza crust, homemade (page 233) or purchased

½   cup Fresh Tomato Salsa (page 71) or good-quality purchased tomato salsa

2   cups grated Monterey Jack cheese

1   cup canned black beans, drained and rinsed

2   tablespoons chopped cilantro or parsley

1   cup corn kernels, fresh or frozen

½   cup chopped red bell pepper

½   cup sliced black olives

GREEK PIZZA WITH FETA

Serves 4

Offer this pizza with a lively topping of red onion, spinach, cheeses, and pine nuts for a variety of flavors at a pizza party.

Preheat oven to 450°F. Place crust on a pizza pan or baking sheet. Spread crust with sauce to ½ inch from the edge. Add onion, spinach, and parsley. Sprinkle with oregano, salt, and pepper. Spoon dollops of ricotta on top. Sprinkle with feta and pine nuts. Bake until crust is crisp and topping is bubbly, about 10 minutes. Transfer to a cutting board and, using a pizza-cutting wheel or sharp knife, slice into 8 wedges.

1   12-inch pizza crust, homemade (page 233) or purchased

½   cup pizza sauce, homemade (page 233) or purchased

½   cup chopped red onion

1   package (10 ounces) frozen spinach, thawed and squeezed dry

1   tablespoon chopped fresh parsley

¼   teaspoon dried oregano

¼   teaspoon salt

Freshly ground pepper to taste

1   cup ricotta cheese or cottage cheese

1   cup crumbled feta cheese

2   tablespoons pine nuts

FOUR-CHEESE PIZZA
Serves 4

This is for my two teenage grandsons, who will only eat pizzas topped with sauce and cheese. This ought to cover it!

Preheat oven to 450°F. Place crust on a pizza pan or baking sheet. Spread crust with sauce to ½ inch from the edge. Sprinkle cheeses on top. Bake until crust is crisp and cheese is melted, and top is bubbly, about 10 minutes. Transfer to a cutting board and, using a pizza-cutting wheel or sharp knife, slice into 8 wedges. Serve immediately.

1   12-inch pizza crust, homemade (page 233) or purchased

½   cup pizza sauce, homemade (page 233) or purchased

½   cup grated mozzarella cheese

½   cup grated Monterey Jack cheese

¼   cup grated provolone cheese

¼   cup grated Parmesan cheese

VEGETABLE PIZZA

Serves 4

You don't have to be a vegetarian to enjoy this garden-fresh pizza.

Preheat oven to 450°F. Place crust on a pizza pan or baking sheet. Spread crust with sauce to ½ inch from the edge. Sprinkle with 1 cup mozzarella cheese. Add mushrooms, onion, bell pepper, and tomatoes. Sprinkle with remaining mozzarella cheese and Parmesan. Bake until crust is crisp and topping is bubbly, about 10 minutes. Transfer to a cutting board and, using a pizza-cutting wheel or sharp knife, slice into 8 wedges. Serve immediately.

1	12-inch pizza crust, homemade (page 233) or purchased
½	cup pizza sauce, homemade (page 233) or purchased
2	cups grated mozzarella cheese
4	ounces mushrooms, sliced
1	cup chopped yellow onion
1	cup chopped green bell pepper
2	plum (Roma) tomatoes, thinly sliced
	Freshly grated Parmesan cheese for sprinkling on top

STiR-FRiES

CHAPTER 13

HEALTHFUL MEALS IN MINUTES

Stir-frying is ideal for quick and easy suppers. Most of the ingredients take some prepping, but the actual cooking time is short and supper can be ready in minutes. It is a healthful technique because only a small amount of oil is used and butter is not added. The basic elements of stir-fries are taste, texture, and color.

Stir-frying is an ancient Asian method of cooking. It is simply tossing and stirring uniformly sized food quickly in hot oil over high heat until meat is cooked and vegetables are tender-crisp. Most stir-fry dishes are served with rice or Asian noodles and additional soy sauce on the side.

STIR-FRY BASICS

EQUIPMENT

The only equipment needed is a wok or a large skillet, a ladle, a spatula, and a sharp knife. A wok is authentic and fun to use, but not necessary. A large nonstick skillet works very well on a conventional stove top, as long as it is large enough to accommodate the ingredients with room for tossing. Chopsticks are fun but optional (unless you are an expert, you'll eat a lot more slowly).

INGREDIENTS

The main ingredients for stir-fries are meats, vegetables, shellfish, and sometimes fish. Peanut oil is recommended for frying because of its high smoking point, but vegetable oil can also be used.

HELPFUL STIR-FRYING TIPS

- Assemble all tools and ingredients before starting.
- Cut ingredients into uniform bite-sized pieces.
- Heat wok or skillet over high heat and add oil. Do not start to cook until oil is hot but not smoking.
- Add ingredients and toss and stir constantly. It only takes a few minutes.
- Add marinade and stir until thickened.
- Serve immediately with rice or noodles.

Included here are a variety of stir-fry dishes such as Beef and Vegetable Stir-Fry (facing page); Chicken, Mushroom, and Cashew Stir-Fry (page 253); Sweet-and-Sour Pork Stir-Fry (page 255); and Shrimp, Asparagus, and Mushroom Stir-Fry (page 257).

BEEF AND VEGETABLE STIR-FRY

Serves 4

This dish is full of vegetables for a healthful, complete meal that will fit into any weeknight supper menu. Have all ingredients prepared before you start to cook. Rice is a natural accompaniment.

¼	cup soy sauce
1½	tablespoons red wine vinegar
1	tablespoon cornstarch
1	large garlic clove, minced
1	tablespoon peeled, grated fresh ginger or ¼ teaspoon ground ginger
1	pound top sirloin, cut into ⅜-by-1½-inch-long strips (see Note)
3	tablespoons peanut oil
2	cups small broccoli florets
4	ounces mushrooms, sliced
4	green onions, including some tender green tops, sliced
½	red bell pepper, seeded and cut into ½-by-2-inch strips
2	tablespoons water

In a large bowl, mix together soy sauce, vinegar, cornstarch, garlic, and ginger. Add meat, toss to coat, and let stand at room temperature for 10 minutes.

In a wok or large skillet over medium-high heat, warm 1½ tablespoons oil. When oil is hot, remove meat from marinade with a slotted spoon and add to wok. Reserve marinade. Stir-fry meat until browned, about 4 minutes. Transfer to a plate.

Add remaining 1½ tablespoons oil to the wok. When oil is hot, add broccoli, mushrooms, green onions, and bell pepper and stir-fry for 3 minutes. Add water, cover, and cook until vegetables are tender-crisp, about 3 minutes.

Return meat to wok along with reserved marinade and stir-fry until heated through and sauce is thickened, 2 to 3 minutes. Serve immediately.

NOTE: Placing the meat in the freezer for 15 minutes before cutting will make it easier to slice.

GINGER BEEF, ASPARAGUS, AND GARLIC STIR-FRY

Serves 4

Flank steak cooks quickly and evenly because of its firm texture and thin cut and works well in stir-fries. Here it is combined with asparagus and onions in a flavorful sauce.

In a large bowl, whisk together hoisin sauce, soy sauce, wine, cornstarch, ginger, and garlic. Add meat, toss to coat, and let stand at room temperature for 10 minutes.

In a wok or large skillet over medium-high heat, warm 1 tablespoon oil. When oil is hot, remove meat from marinade with a slotted spoon and add to wok. Reserve marinade. Stir-fry meat until browned on the outside but slightly pink on the inside, about 5 minutes. Transfer to a plate.

Add remaining 1 tablespoon oil to the wok. When oil is hot, add asparagus and onion and stir-fry until vegetables are tender-crisp, about 5 minutes. Return meat to wok along with reserved marinade and stir-fry until heated through and sauce is thickened, 2 to 3 minutes.

1	tablespoon hoisin sauce
1	tablespoon soy sauce
¼	cup dry white wine
1	tablespoon cornstarch
1	tablespoon peeled, chopped fresh ginger or 1 teaspoon ground ginger
2	garlic cloves, minced
1	flank steak (about 1½ pounds), sliced on the diagonal across the grain into ½-inch strips (see Note, page 249)
2	tablespoons peanut oil
¾	pound asparagus, tough ends removed and cut on the diagonal into ½-inch pieces
½	cup chopped yellow onion

FLANK STEAK AND TOMATO STIR-FRY

Serves 4

Crispy vegetables complement the tender, juicy flank steak
in this quick stir-fry supper dish.

In a large bowl, whisk together soy sauce, wine, garlic, and cornstarch. Add steak, toss to coat, and let stand at room temperature for 10 minutes.

In a wok or large skillet over medium-high heat, warm 1½ tablespoons oil. When oil is hot, remove meat from the marinade with a slotted spoon and add to wok. Reserve marinade. Stir-fry meat until browned on the outside and slightly pink on the inside, 3 to 4 minutes. Transfer to a plate.

Add remaining 1½ tablespoons oil to the wok. When oil is hot, add celery and bell pepper and stir-fry, until tender-crisp, about 5 minutes. Add tomatoes and stir-fry 1 minute longer. Return meat to wok along with reserved marinade and stir-fry until heated through and sauce is thickened, 2 to 3 minutes longer. Serve immediately with rice or noodles.

⅓ cup soy sauce

2 tablespoons dry white wine or water

1 garlic clove, minced

1 tablespoon cornstarch

1½ pounds flank steak, cut on the diagonal across the grain into ½-by-2-inch strips (see Note, page 249)

3 tablespoons peanut oil

2 celery stalks, sliced on the diagonal into ¾-inch slices

1 green bell pepper, seeded and cut into 1-inch pieces

2 plum (Roma) tomatoes, cut into eight wedges

Rice or soba noodles, cooked according to package directions and drained, for serving

BEEF TERIYAKI STIR-FRY

Serves 4

Several hours must be allowed for the beef to marinate in this easy all-meat stir-fry entrée. Serve with noodles or steamed rice and a plate of crisp sliced cucumbers.

In a large bowl, whisk together broth, soy sauce, cornstarch, vinegar, and garlic. Add meat and toss to coat. Cover and marinate 2 to 3 hours in the refrigerator, stirring once.

In a wok or large skillet over medium-high heat, warm 1 tablespoon oil. When oil is hot, remove meat from the marinade with a slotted spoon and add to the wok. Reserve marinade. Stir-fry meat until browned on the outside and slightly pink on the inside, 3 to 4 minutes. Add more oil if needed. Add reserved marinade to the wok and stir-fry until sauce is thickened, 2 to 3 minutes. Serve over rice, topped with green onions.

¼ cup beef broth

¼ cup soy sauce

1 tablespoon cornstarch

1 tablespoon rice wine vinegar or white wine vinegar

1 garlic clove, minced

1½ pounds top sirloin, cut into ½-by-2-inch strips (see Note, page 249)

1 to 2 tablespoons peanut oil

1 cup long-grain white rice, cooked according to package directions (3 cups cooked)

4 or 5 green onions, including some tender green tops, sliced

CHICKEN, MUSHROOM, AND CASHEW STIR-FRY

Serves 4

Hoisin sauce is an Asian condiment made from soybeans, garlic, chile peppers, and other spices. It adds a sweet and spicy flavor to stir-fry dishes. It can be purchased in jars at well-stocked supermarkets. Serve this classic combination of chicken and cashew nuts with noodles.

2	tablespoons hoisin sauce
1	tablespoon soy sauce
2	tablespoons water
1	tablespoon cornstarch
3	boned and skinned chicken breast halves (about 1½ pounds), cut into ½-by-2-inch strips
3	tablespoons peanut oil
1	large garlic clove, halved
1	1-inch piece of fresh ginger, peeled and halved
4	ounces mushrooms, sliced
½	red bell pepper, seeded and cut into ½-inch strips
3	green onions, including some tender green tops, sliced
¼	cup cashew halves
1	package (6 ounces) Asian noodles, cooked according to package directions and drained

In a large bowl, whisk together hoisin sauce, soy sauce, water, and cornstarch. Add chicken, toss to coat, and let stand at room temperature for 10 minutes.

In a wok or large skillet over medium-high heat, warm 2 tablespoons oil. When oil is hot, add garlic and ginger and stir-fry until fragrant, stirring constantly, about 30 seconds. Remove garlic and ginger and discard. Remove chicken from marinade with a slotted spoon and add to wok. Reserve marinade. Stir-fry until chicken turns white, 3 to 4 minutes. Transfer to a plate.

Add remaining 1 tablespoon oil to the wok. When oil is hot, add mushrooms, bell pepper, and green onions and stir-fry until tender-crisp, about 5 minutes. Return chicken to wok along with the reserved marinade and stir-fry until heated through and sauce is thickened, 2 to 3 minutes. Stir in cashews and serve immediately with noodles.

CHICKEN, MUSHROOM, AND RED BELL PEPPER STIR-FRY

Serves 4

Supper is a breeze with this chicken stir-fry with mushrooms and crunchy celery. Serve over rice or noodles.

In a large bowl, whisk together soy sauce, sherry, cornstarch, ginger, and garlic. Add chicken, toss to coat, and let stand at room temperature for 10 minutes.

In a wok or large skillet over medium-high heat, warm 1½ tablespoons oil. When oil is hot, remove chicken from marinade with a slotted spoon and add to wok. Reserve marinade. Stir-fry until chicken turns white, 3 to 4 minutes. Transfer to a plate.

Add remaining 1½ tablespoons oil to the wok. When oil is hot, add mushrooms, celery, and bell pepper and stir-fry until vegetables are tender-crisp, about 5 minutes. Return chicken to wok along with the reserved marinade and stir-fry until heated through and sauce is thickened, 2 to 3 minutes longer. Sprinkle with chopped green onion. Serve immediately, passing additional soy sauce.

2   tablespoons soy sauce, plus extra for serving

2   tablespoons sherry or dry white wine

2   teaspoons cornstarch

1   teaspoon peeled, grated fresh ginger or ¼ teaspoon ground ginger

1   large garlic clove, minced

3   boned and skinned chicken breast halves (about 1½ pounds), cut into bite-sized pieces

3   tablespoons peanut oil

4   ounces mushrooms, sliced

2   celery stalks, cut on the diagonal into ½-inch slices

½   red bell pepper, seeded and cut into ½-inch pieces

6   green onions, including some tender green tops, chopped for sprinkling on top

SWEET-AND-SOUR PORK STIR-FRY

Serves 4

Pineapple and pork are a classic combination in this stir-fry. Serve with rice or soba noodles. Water chestnuts add extra crunch and flavor.

In a large bowl, whisk together reserved pineapple juice, vinegar, soy sauce, and cornstarch. Add pork, toss to coat, and let stand at room temperature for 10 minutes.

In a wok or large skillet over medium-high heat, warm 1½ tablespoons oil. When oil is hot, remove pork from marinade with a slotted spoon and add to wok. Reserve marinade. Stir-fry pork until lightly browned, about 5 minutes. Transfer to a plate.

Add remaining 1½ tablespoons oil to the wok. When oil is hot, add bell pepper, onion, celery, and garlic and stir-fry until vegetables are tender-crisp, about 5 minutes. Stir in water chestnuts and pineapple chunks. Return pork to wok along with reserved marinade and stir-fry until heated through and sauce is thickened, 2 to 3 minutes longer.

1	can (8 ounces) pineapple chunks, drained (reserve juice)
1	tablespoon white wine vinegar
2	tablespoons soy sauce
1	tablespoon cornstarch
1	pound pork shoulder, cut into 1-inch pieces
3	tablespoons peanut oil
½	large green bell pepper, seeded and cut into ¾-inch pieces
½	cup chopped yellow onion
2	celery stalks, cut on the diagonal into ¾-inch slices
1	garlic clove, minced
½	cup sliced water chestnuts, drained

PORK STIR-FRY WITH BELL PEPPERS, SUGAR SNAP PEAS, AND PEANUTS

Serves 4

Beat the clock with this easy stir-fry combination of contrasting colors and textures topped with peanuts.

In a large bowl, whisk together soy sauce, broth, vinegar, and cornstarch. Add pork, toss to coat, and let stand at room temperature for 10 minutes.

In a wok or large skillet over medium-high heat, warm 1½ tablespoons oil. When oil is hot, remove pork from marinade with a slotted spoon and add to wok. Reserve marinade. Stir-fry until pork is no longer pink, about 3 minutes. Transfer to a plate.

Add remaining 1½ tablespoons oil to wok. When oil is hot, add bell pepper, peas, and green onions and stir-fry, until tender-crisp, about 5 minutes. Return the meat to the wok along with the reserved marinade and stir-fry until heated through and sauce is thickened, 2 to 3 minutes longer. Serve over rice, sprinkled with peanuts.

2	tablespoons soy sauce
¼	cup chicken broth
2	tablespoons red wine vinegar
1	tablespoon cornstarch
1	pound boneless pork, cut into ½-inch strips
3	tablespoons peanut oil
½	red or green bell pepper, seeded and cut into ½-by-2-inch strips
1	cup sugar snap peas, trimmed and halved
3	green onions, including some tender green tops, sliced
1	cup long-grain white rice, cooked according to package directions (3 cups cooked)
½	cup chopped unsalted peanuts

SHRIMP, ASPARAGUS, AND MUSHROOM STIR-FRY

Serves 4

Shrimp is ideal in stir-fries, as it cooks beautifully in seconds, while in other methods it can easily be overcooked and become tough. Here it is especially good combined with asparagus and mushrooms.

In a medium bowl, whisk together soy sauce, sherry, garlic, cornstarch, and ginger. Add shrimp, toss to coat, and let stand at room temperature for 10 minutes.

In a wok or large skillet over medium-high heat, warm 1½ tablespoons oil. When oil is hot, remove shrimp from marinade with a slotted spoon and add to wok. Reserve marinade. Stir-fry until shrimp turns pink, about 2 minutes. Transfer to a plate.

Add remaining 1½ tablespoons oil to wok. When oil is hot, add asparagus, green onions, and mushrooms and stir-fry until vegetables are tender, about 5 minutes. Return shrimp to wok along with reserved marinade and stir-fry until heated through and sauce is thickened, 2 to 3 minutes. Serve immediately.

¼   cup soy sauce

2   tablespoons sherry or dry white wine

1   garlic clove, minced

2   teaspoons cornstarch

1   slice peeled fresh ginger, chopped or ½ teaspoon ground ginger

¾   pound large shrimp, peeled and deveined

3   tablespoons peanut oil

½   pound asparagus, tough ends snapped off and cut on the diagonal into ¾-inch pieces

4   green onions, including some tender green tops, sliced

4   ounces mushrooms, sliced

GRILLING

CHAPTER 14

FUN AND CASUAL SUPPERS

Grilling is one of the easiest ways to prepare supper. It means less fuss, less fat, more flavor, and more fun.

Grilling is not limited to just the summer season. In some areas, the backyard grill has become the outdoor kitchen for year-round use. Grilling is a good family activity as well as a casual and informal way to entertain friends.

GRILLING BASICS

EQUIPMENT

Outdoor grill. Gas, charcoal, and electric are all good options. Follow manufacturer's directions carefully. Keep an extra propane tank on hand for gas grilling.
Briquettes for charcoal grill. (Use only the best quality.)

HELPFUL TOOLS

Other useful tools for grilling are a long-handled spatula; tongs and a long-handled fork; an insulated oven mitt; an instant-read meat thermometer; a basting brush; metal and bamboo skewers (see Note below); and a wire brush for cleaning the grill grate. A small side table nearby to hold food, seasonings, basting sauce, tools, and serving dishes makes grilling more convenient. A weather-proof grill cover will protect your grill from the elements.

NOTE: Bamboo skewers are used for lighter ingredients such as vegetables and fruits. Flat metal skewers are best for meats and kabobs. If using bamboo skewers, soak them in water 30 minutes before grilling to prevent them from burning.

GRILLING TECHNIQUES

PREHEATING: Preheat charcoal briquettes for 20 to 30 minutes and gas and electric grills for 5 to 10 minutes. An electric coil starter or metal chimney is recommended for lighting briquettes. While charcoal lighter fluid and quick-lighting briquettes speed the process, they often leave an aftertaste.

TEMPERATURE CONTROL: Direct and indirect cooking are the two ways to cook food on the grill. Direct grilling is similar to broiling. The food is placed directly over the heat source. This method is used for foods that cook for less than 25 minutes, i.e., steaks, chops, burgers, chicken pieces, and some fish. Indirect grilling is similar to roasting. The food is placed on the cooler areas of the grill. This method is used for foods that require slower cooking times, such as roasts, ribs, whole chickens, whole fish, and tougher cuts of meat. The use of a meat thermometer is helpful when cooking for longer periods of time.

FLAVORING THE COALS: For an extra-smoky flavor in a charcoal grill, soak a few wood chips in water for about an hour, drain, and add to the coals during the last 15 minutes of cooking time. Fresh herbs or citrus peel can also be added to the coals for extra flavor and fragrance.

MARINADES, SAUCES, BASTES, AND RUBS

Marinades enhance flavor, seal in juices, keep food moist, and in some cases, tenderize. Use nonreactive containers such as glass, ceramic, or stainless steel to marinate. Marinades can be a single ingredient, such as teriyaki sauce or balsamic vinegar, or a combination of flavorful ingredients, such as assorted herbs, oils, vinegars, citrus juices, and wine. Food needs to marinate 2 to 3 hours or even overnight to allow the flavors to be absorbed. The exception is fish, which should only be marinated 15 to 20 minutes, especially if a citrus marinade is used, because the acid breaks down the fibers and the fish will begin to "cook." Remove foods from the marinade before grilling. If using the marinade to baste or to serve as a sauce after grilling, it is important to boil it for 1 minute to destroy any bacteria from contact with raw meat.

Sauces are brushed on during grilling to add color and flavor. There are many sauces; the most popular is barbecue sauce, usually a sweet, tomato-based sauce with seasonings. It burns easily and should be added toward the end of the grilling time.

Bastes are used to brush on food as it cooks, to keep it from drying out. They can be a single ingredient, such as melted butter, stock, wine, or boiled leftover marinade.

Rubs are a combination of dry seasonings rubbed on the food several hours before grilling. They add texture and boost flavor.

HELPFUL GRILLING TIPS

- Do prep work in advance and assemble all tools before starting to grill.
- Be sure your grill is really clean before grilling.
- Locate the grill a safe distance from the house and from any combustible materials.
- Do not start to grill food until the grill is totally heated.
- Do not spray or oil a hot grill; brush the food with oil instead.
- Do not leave the grill unattended while grilling.
- Brush on barbecue sauce and other sweet sauces at the end of cooking time to prevent burning.
- Do not overcrowd the grill—and don't turn the food too often; usually once is enough.
- Do not use water for controlling flare-ups; move the food to a cooler spot, close the grill, or turn off the gas.
- When through grilling, close or turn off the grill. When it is cool, clean grill grate with a wire brush. Cover the grill with the grill cover when not in use.

This chapter features many classics, from steaks to chicken breasts, as well as Asian-Style Grilled Pork Chops (page 273), Ribs with Really Good Barbecue Sauce (page 275), Kabobs from the Sea (page 291), and a variety of recipes for grilled fresh vegetables.

GRILLED MARINATED BEEF ROAST

Serves 8

Allow the meat to marinate in this flavorful marinade several hours or overnight, then slowly roast in a covered grill, maintaining a constant medium heat. Serve with Pasta and Vegetable Salad with Creamy Dill Dressing (page 63). Leftover roast can be used for sandwiches or Continental Salad (page 28).

Place meat in a large glass baking dish. In a small bowl or cup, whisk together marinade ingredients. Pour over meat and turn meat to coat. Cover and marinate in the refrigerator 4 to 6 hours or up to overnight, turning several times. Bring roast to room temperature before grilling.

Preheat grill. Remove meat from marinade. In a small saucepan, boil marinade for 1 minute. Grill roast over medium heat with cover closed, basting several times, until meat thermometer registers 150°F for medium, about 1 hour. Transfer to a cutting board and let stand for 10 minutes before carving.

1 top sirloin roast, 1½ inches thick (about 4 pounds)

SOY-WINE MARINADE

¼ cup soy sauce

¼ cup dry red wine

1 tablespoon red wine vinegar

1 tablespoon Worcestershire sauce

1 teaspoon ground ginger

1 teaspoon ground mustard

2 garlic cloves, minced

¼ teaspoon salt

Freshly ground pepper to taste

GRILLED NEW YORK STEAKS WITH CREAMY HORSERADISH SAUCE

Serves 4

Time to splurge and have steak for a barbecue supper. New York steak is popular because it has more flavor and is more tender than some of the other meat cuts. With this rub, the steaks come out juicy and delicious. Creamy Horseradish Sauce makes a complementary topping. For salad, try the Mixed Greens, Avocado, and Mushroom Salad with Tangy Red Dressing (page 51).

Place steaks on a large plate. In a cup or small bowl, whisk together olive oil, garlic, salt, and pepper. Spread mixture on both sides of steaks, pressing to adhere with the back of a spoon. Let stand at room temperature for 15 minutes.

Preheat grill. Grill steaks over high heat, turning once, until medium-rare, 4 to 5 minutes on each side. Let stand for 5 minutes before serving. Serve with Creamy Horseradish Sauce.

4	New York steaks, 1¼ inches thick (6 to 8 ounces each)
3	tablespoons olive oil
2	garlic cloves, minced
1	tablespoon coarse salt
½	teaspoon freshly ground pepper
	Creamy Horseradish Sauce (recipe follows)

CREAMY HORSERADISH SAUCE

In a small bowl, mix together all ingredients.

Makes about ½ cup

¼	cup mayonnaise
¼	cup sour cream or plain nonfat yogurt
1	tablespoon prepared horseradish
1	teaspoon Worcestershire sauce
¼	teaspoon ground mustard

GRILLED WINE-MARINATED FLANK STEAK

Serves 4

Flank steak is a popular choice for grilling, because it cooks quickly and is full of flavor. It needs to steep in this wine marinade for several hours to tenderize and absorb the flavors. Serve with Corn on the Cob with Lime Butter (page 214).

In a large glass baking dish, whisk together oil, wine, vinegar, garlic, Worcestershire sauce, Tabasco, salt, and pepper. Add steak and turn to coat. Cover and refrigerate for several hours, turning once. Bring to room temperature before grilling.

Preheat grill. Remove steak from marinade and discard marinade. Grill steak over high heat, turning once, until medium-rare, 6 to 8 minutes on each side. (Flank steak will be most tender when grilled to rare or medium-rare.) Transfer to a cutting board and let stand for 5 minutes. Slice meat on the diagonal across the grain and transfer to a platter. Serve immediately.

1	tablespoon vegetable oil
1/4	cup dry red wine
1	tablespoon red wine vinegar
2	garlic cloves, minced
1	teaspoon Worcestershire sauce
2	to 3 drops Tabasco sauce
1/4	teaspoon salt
	Freshly ground pepper to taste
1	flank steak (1½ to 2 pounds)

GRILLED FLANK STEAK IN SOY MARINADE

Serves 4

Here's an easy way to bring Asian flavors to the table. Include Fried Rice (page 198) and Exotic Fruit Salad (page 61).

In a large glass baking dish, whisk together soy sauce, honey, vinegar, Worcestershire sauce, olive oil, garlic, and ginger. Add steak and turn to coat. Cover and refrigerate for several hours, turning once. Bring to room temperature before grilling.

Preheat grill. Remove steak from marinade and discard marinade. Grill steak over high heat, turning once, until medium-rare, 6 to 8 minutes on each side. Transfer to a cutting board and let stand for 5 minutes. Slice on the diagonal across the grain and transfer to a platter. Garnish with green onions and serve immediately.

¼ cup soy sauce

2 tablespoons honey

2 tablespoons balsamic vinegar or red wine vinegar

1 teaspoon Worcestershire sauce

2 tablespoons olive oil

2 garlic cloves, minced

1 teaspoon ground ginger

1 flank steak (1½ to 2 pounds)

½ cup chopped green onions, including some tender green tops

GRILLED BEEF FAJITAS
Serves 4

At a Mexican restaurant, the meat comes sizzling on a hot griddle to the table. You can create the same effect by grilling the meat and serving it very hot, along with sautéed bell peppers. Everyone assembles their own fajitas at the table.

Add meat to marinade, cover, and refrigerate 1 to 2 hours, turning several times. Bring to room temperature before grilling.

In a large skillet over medium heat, warm oil. Add bell peppers and onion and sauté until vegetables are tender, 6 to 8 minutes. Set aside and keep warm.

Preheat grill. Remove meat from marinade. In a small saucepan, boil marinade for 1 minute. Grill meat over high heat, turning once and basting occasionally with marinade, until medium-rare, 4 to 5 minutes on each side. Transfer to a cutting board and let stand for 5 minutes. Slice on the diagonal across the grain. Serve meat and vegetables on a platter along with warm tortillas.

Instruct diners to assemble their own fajitas: Place several strips of meat on a tortilla. Add some bell pepper–onion mixture and a spoonful each of grated cheese and sour cream. Roll up, top with a spoonful of salsa, and garnish with avocado slices.

1	top sirloin steak (about 1 pound)
	Lime Marinade (recipe on facing page)
2	tablespoons vegetable oil
1	red bell pepper, seeded and cut into narrow strips
1	green bell pepper, seeded and cut into narrow strips
1	small yellow onion, sliced
8	10-inch flour tortillas, warmed (see Note, page 70)
1	cup grated Monterey Jack cheese
½	cup sour cream
½	cup Fresh Tomato Salsa (page 71) or good-quality purchased tomato salsa
1	avocado, sliced, for garnish

LIME MARINADE

In a large bowl, whisk together all ingredients.

Makes about ½ cup

Juice of 1 lime
⅓ cup dry white wine
1 teaspoon Worcestershire sauce
2 tablespoons vegetable oil
1 garlic clove, minced
½ teaspoon dried oregano
¼ teaspoon ground cumin
¼ teaspoon salt
⅛ teaspoon freshly ground pepper

BEEF-VEGETABLE KABOBS

Serves 6

Kabobs are composed of cubes of food threaded on skewers and grilled, with frequent turning and basting. They are fun to make and fun to eat. Here, cubes of tender, marinated beef are alternated with vegetables on skewers for an appealing entrée. Serve with a Summer Salad Bowl (page 57).

In a bowl large enough to hold the beef, stir together marinade ingredients. Reserve $1/3$ cup of marinade for basting. Add beef to the bowl and mix well. Cover and marinate for several hours in the refrigerator, stirring several times. Bring to room temperature before grilling.

Preheat grill. Remove beef from marinade and discard marinade. Thread meat on skewers, alternating with vegetables. Grill over medium heat, turning often and brushing with reserved marinade, until beef is medium-rare and vegetables are tender-crisp, 8 to 10 minutes. Serve immediately.

MARINADE

1   cup flat beer

6   green onions, including some tender green tops, chopped

2   garlic cloves, chopped

$1/2$ cup soy sauce

1   tablespoon fresh lemon juice

1   tablespoon firmly packed brown sugar

1   tablespoon peeled and chopped fresh ginger or $1/2$ teaspoon ground ginger

2   pounds top sirloin, cut into $1 1/2$-inch squares (see Note, page 249)

1   green bell pepper, seeded and cut into 1-inch pieces

1   red bell pepper, seeded and cut into 1-inch pieces

1   yellow onion, cut into 1-inch wedges and separated

2   zucchini, unpeeled, cut into $3/4$-inch slices

12   cherry tomatoes

12   large mushrooms, stems removed

GRILLED CABIN BURGERS

Serves 4

This hamburger topped with bacon, cheese, and tomato is a favorite with the grandkids. Add condiments of your choice and serve with Potato Wedges (page 220).

Preheat grill. In a large bowl, combine the beef, Worcestershire sauce, Tabasco, and salt and pepper. Shape into 4 patties. Brush patties on both sides with oil and grill over high heat, turning once, until well done, 4 to 5 minutes on each side. Place cheese slices on top of patties the last minute or two of cooking time.

Warm buns on grill until lightly toasted. Serve burgers in buns with a bacon strip, tomato slices, an onion slice, and a lettuce leaf on each. Pass the condiments.

1¼ pounds ground beef

1 teaspoon Worcestershire sauce

2 or 3 drops Tabasco sauce, or to taste

Salt and freshly ground pepper

Vegetable oil for brushing on patties

4 slices Swiss cheese

4 large buns, split

4 bacon strips, halved, cooked crisp, and drained

1 tomato, thinly sliced

4 red onion slices

4 lettuce leaves

CONDIMENTS

Mayonnaise

Mustard

Ketchup

Relish

MUSTARDY GRILLED PORK CHOPS

Serves 4

Thick pork chops simply brushed with a mustard baste and cooked on the grill bring spectacular results. Offer Smashed Potatoes with Blue Cheese and Chives (page 217) as a side dish.

In a small bowl, whisk together mustard, vinegar, honey, thyme, olive oil, salt, and pepper. Place pork chops on a plate and brush with mustard mixture on both sides. Let stand at room temperature for 30 minutes.

Preheat grill. Grill chops over medium heat, turning once, until lightly browned and slightly pink on the inside, 6 to 8 minutes on each side.

2	tablespoons Dijon mustard
2	tablespoons red wine vinegar
1	teaspoon honey
½	teaspoon dried thyme
2	tablespoons olive oil
¼	teaspoon salt
	Freshly ground pepper to taste
4	boneless pork chops, 1 inch thick (1½ to 2 pounds)

ASIAN-STYLE GRILLED PORK CHOPS
Serves 4

These mellow pork chops are brushed with a sweet hoisin glaze for an outstanding flavor. Serve with rice or noodles.

Preheat grill. Brush pork chops lightly with oil on both sides. Season generously with salt and pepper. Grill chops over medium heat, turning once, until lightly browned and slightly pink on the inside, about 6 minutes on each side. Brush tops with glaze and grill 1 minute longer. Turn chops, brush other side with glaze, and grill 1 minute longer. Transfer to a plate and sprinkle with green onions.

4	boneless pork chops, 1 inch thick (1½ to 2 pounds)
	Vegetable oil for brushing
	Salt and freshly ground pepper to taste
	Hoisin Glaze (recipe follows)
¼	cup chopped green onions, including some tender green tops

HOISIN GLAZE

In a small bowl, mix together all ingredients.

Makes about ½ cup

¼	cup hoisin sauce
3	tablespoons ketchup
2	tablespoons white wine vinegar
¼	teaspoon ground ginger
1	tablespoon soy sauce

GRILLED HONEY-MUSTARD PORK TENDERLOIN

Serves 6 to 8

For a special supper, serve tender, juicy pork tenderloins with a honey-sweetened mustard sauce. You should plan ahead so the pork can marinate several hours. Serve with Strawberry-Pineapple Delight (page 319) for dessert.

Place pork in a large glass baking dish. In a medium bowl, whisk together remaining ingredients, except parsley. Set aside ½ cup marinade for sauce. Pour remaining marinade over pork and turn to coat. Cover and refrigerate for several hours, turning occasionally. Bring to room temperature before grilling.

Preheat grill. Remove pork from marinade and discard marinade. Grill over medium heat, turning once, until pork is slightly pink on the inside and an instant-read thermometer registers 155°F, 45 to 50 minutes. Let stand for 5 to 10 minutes before slicing.

In a small saucepan over medium heat, warm reserved sauce. Arrange pork slices on a platter, spread with the sauce, and garnish with parsley.

2   pork tenderloins (1 to 1½ pounds each)
½   cup honey
½   cup Dijon mustard
2   tablespoons dry white wine
1   teaspoon Worcestershire sauce
¼   teaspoon salt
    Freshly ground pepper to taste
    Fresh parsley sprigs for garnish

RIBS WITH REALLY GOOD BARBECUE SAUCE

Serves 4

Summer is the time for a supper of classic ribs on the patio. Serve with Best Coleslaw (page 55), Four-Bean Bake (page 201), and garlic bread for a traditional ribs dinner. Use a covered grill for best results.

Preheat grill. Arrange ribs in a single layer on a lightly sprayed or oiled 12-by-16½-inch aluminum-foil pan, bone side down. Pour 1 cup sauce over ribs. Place pan holding ribs on grill over medium heat and cook, with cover closed, for 1 hour and 45 minutes, basting occasionally with sauce. If pan starts to dry out, add more sauce. Remove ribs from the pan and place directly on grill, bone side down. Grill until meat is very tender, 15 to 20 minutes longer, basting several times with remaining sauce.

4   pounds baby back ribs, membrane removed (see Note), cut into serving pieces (2 or 3 ribs each)
    Tangy Barbecue Sauce (recipe follows)

NOTE: Removing the membrane is an important step. It allows the sauce to penetrate the meat and the fat to drip away during grilling. On the underside (bone side) of the ribs, loosen the white membrane with the point of a knife and make a slit large enough so that you can insert your finger under the membrane and pull it up and away from the ribs. Using a towel helps grip the membrane. Carefully peel back the membrane at an angle. You may need to start over once or twice before you are successful, but it is worth the effort. (Some butchers will remove the membrane for you.)

TANGY BARBECUE SAUCE

This is an all-purpose sauce, good on ribs, chicken, and other meats.

In a medium saucepan over medium heat, whisk together all ingredients and simmer, uncovered, until flavors are blended, 6 to 7 minutes.

Makes about 2 cups

1   cup flat beer
1   cup ketchup
1   tablespoon Worcestershire sauce
2   tablespoons soy sauce
1   tablespoon honey
    Juice of ½ lemon
1   garlic clove, minced
    Freshly ground pepper to taste

GRILLED HAM SLICE

Serves 4

A thick ham slice is delicious when quickly seared on the grill. Here, a mustard-honey spread is brushed on the ham for more flavor. Cheesy Potatoes (page 218) goes well with the ham.

Preheat grill. In a small bowl, whisk together mustard, honey, and cloves. Brush ham with mustard sauce on both sides and grill over medium heat, turning once, until heated through, about 10 minutes.

2   tablespoons Dijon mustard

1   tablespoon honey

¼   teaspoon ground cloves

1   cooked ham slice, ½ inch thick (about 1¼ pounds)

GRILLED ROSEMARY LAMB CHOPS
Serves 4

Lamb chops are a small cut with big flavor. Allow 2 chops per serving and marinate 1 to 2 hours. This method of grilling will guarantee moist and juicy chops every time. Serve with a Chopped Greek Salad (page 56).

In a cup or small bowl, whisk together all marinade ingredients. Place lamb chops in a glass baking dish and pour marinade over. Cover and marinate for 1 to 2 hours in the refrigerator, turning several times. Bring to room temperature before grilling.

Preheat grill. Remove chops from marinade and discard marinade. Stand chops upright on grill on the bone end and grill over medium heat for 5 minutes. Then lay chops on one side and grill 5 minutes longer. Turn chops, and grill 5 minutes longer for medium-rare. Garnish with rosemary sprigs and serve immediately.

MARINADE

1	tablespoon olive oil
¼	cup dry white wine
1	tablespoon fresh lemon juice
1	tablespoon fresh chopped rosemary or 1 teaspoon dried rosemary
2	garlic cloves, minced
¼	teaspoon salt
	Freshly ground pepper to taste
8	lamb chops, 1 to 1½ inches thick (about 3 pounds), trimmed
	Fresh rosemary sprigs for garnish

GRILLED MAPLE-GLAZED CHICKEN BREASTS

Serves 4 to 6

This chicken gets its sweet taste from a maple glaze. Parmesan-Pecan Rice (page 195) makes an easy, complementary side dish.

Preheat grill. In a small bowl, whisk together glaze ingredients. Season chicken with salt and pepper and brush glaze generously on all sides. Grill chicken breasts over medium heat, turning once, until no longer pink in the center, 6 to 8 minutes on each side.

MAPLE GLAZE

½   cup maple syrup

2   tablespoons ketchup

1   tablespoon red wine vinegar

¼   teaspoon salt

6   boned and skinned chicken breast halves (6 to 8 ounces each)

¼   teaspoon salt

¼   teaspoon freshly ground pepper

GRILLED ORANGE CHICKEN BREASTS
Serves 4 to 6

Grilling is one of the quickest and easiest methods for cooking chicken breasts, but watch carefully as they will soon dry out if overcooked. These breasts are marinated in orange juice, wine, and spices, then grilled until moist and tender. Serve garnished with orange slices.

In an 8-by-10-inch glass baking dish, whisk together orange juice, wine, cloves, ginger, salt, pepper, garlic, oil, and zest. Set aside ¼ cup of the marinade for basting. Add chicken to the dish and turn to coat. Cover and refrigerate for several hours, turning occasionally. Bring to room temperature before grilling.

Preheat grill. Remove chicken from marinade and discard marinade. Grill chicken over medium heat, turning once and basting occasionally with reserved marinade, until no longer pink in the center, 6 to 8 minutes on each side. Garnish with orange segments.

½ cup fresh orange juice

¼ cup dry white wine

¼ teaspoon ground cloves

¼ teaspoon ground ginger

¼ teaspoon salt

Freshly ground pepper to taste

1 garlic clove, minced

1 tablespoon vegetable oil

1 teaspoon grated orange zest

6 boned and skinned chicken breast halves (6 to 8 ounces each)

Orange segments, for garnish

GRILLED LIME-SOY-HONEY CHICKEN BREASTS

Serves 4

Allow several hours for the chicken to marinate in this tasty combination of lime juice, soy sauce, and honey. Serve with Fried Rice (page 198) for a great accompaniment.

In an 8-by-10-inch glass baking dish, whisk together lime juice, soy, honey, and garlic. Add chicken breasts and turn to coat. Cover and marinate in refrigerator for several hours. Bring to room temperature before grilling.

Preheat grill. Remove chicken from marinade and discard marinade. Grill chicken over medium heat, turning once, until no longer pink in the center, 6 to 8 minutes on each side.

Juice of 1 lime
¼ cup soy sauce
1   tablespoon honey
1   garlic clove, minced
4   boned and skinned chicken breast halves
    (6 to 8 ounces each)

CHICKEN AND VEGETABLE KABOBS

Serves 6

Chicken breasts work well for kabobs because they cook evenly and quickly. These kabobs are made with marinated chicken breast pieces and fresh vegetables for a seasonal summer supper.

In a large bowl, whisk together all marinade ingredients. Add vegetables and stir to coat. With a slotted spoon, remove vegetables to a plate and refrigerate. Add chicken to marinade and stir to coat. Cover and marinate for several hours in the refrigerator. Bring chicken and vegetables to room temperature before grilling.

Preheat grill. Remove chicken from marinade. In a small saucepan, boil marinade for 1 minute. Thread chicken pieces on skewers, alternating with vegetables. Grill over medium heat, turning often and brushing with marinade, until chicken is no longer pink in the center and vegetables are tender, about 15 minutes.

LEMON-WINE MARINADE

Juice of 1 lemon
2 tablespoons vegetable oil
2 garlic cloves, minced
¼ cup dry white wine
2 tablespoons soy sauce
1 teaspoon Worcestershire sauce
2 or 3 drops Tabasco sauce
½ teaspoon salt
Freshly ground pepper to taste

12 whole mushrooms, stems removed
1 red bell pepper, cut into 1-inch pieces
1 green bell pepper, cut into 1-inch pieces
½ red onion, cut into chunks
1 zucchini, unpeeled, cut into ½-inch slices
12 cherry tomatoes
4 boned and skinned chicken breast halves (1½ to 2 pounds), cut into large bite-sized pieces

GRILLED GREEK GARLIC CHICKEN LEGS AND THIGHS

Serves 6

If you're looking for something a little different, try these grilled chicken pieces brushed with a lemon-garlic sauce. To round out a Greek menu, serve with Chopped Greek Salad (page 56).

In a large bowl, whisk together lemon juice, garlic, olive oil, wine, oregano, salt, and pepper. Add chicken and turn to coat. Cover and refrigerate several hours, turning once or twice. Bring to room temperature before grilling.

Preheat grill. Remove chicken from marinade. In a small saucepan boil marinade for 1 minute. Grill chicken over medium heat, turning several times and basting occasionally with marinade, until lightly browned and no longer pink in the center, 45 minutes to 1 hour. Transfer chicken to a platter, garnish with olives, and sprinkle with feta cheese.

Juice of 1 lemon
3   garlic cloves, minced
⅓   cup olive oil
⅓   cup dry white wine
1   teaspoon dried oregano
1   teaspoon salt
½   teaspoon freshly ground pepper
6   chicken drumsticks and 6 thighs (about 4 pounds total), excess skin and fat removed
Pitted Kalamata olives or other black olives for garnish
½   cup crumbled feta cheese

NOTE: This chicken can also be baked in the oven at 350°F for about 1 hour.

FAVORITE BARBECUED CHICKEN
Serves 4

Cooking chicken in an aluminum-foil pan right in the sauce is an easy way to prevent burning when grilling chicken with a tomato-based sauce. This sauce can also be used for beef or pork. Serve with corn on the cob.

Preheat grill. In a large bowl, whisk together sauce ingredients. Add chicken and turn to coat.

Place chicken with sauce in an aluminum-foil pan and place the pan on the grill. Grill over medium heat, turning several times, until chicken is no longer pink in the center, about 1 hour. Remove chicken from the pan and place on the grill. Grill until chicken is crispy, turning once, about 10 minutes longer.

ALL-PURPOSE BARBECUE SAUCE

¼	cup ketchup
¼	cup soy sauce
¼	cup dry red wine
1	garlic clove, minced
1	teaspoon Worcestershire sauce
1	tablespoon vegetable oil
2	to 3 drops Tabasco sauce
1	chicken (3 to 3½ pounds), cut into serving pieces or quartered, fat and excess skin removed

GRILLED MUSTARD CHICKEN

Serves 4

If you love mustard, this zesty sauce of two mustards and horseradish is for you. Include Parmesan-Pecan Rice (page 195) and a tossed green salad for a casual supper.

In a small bowl, whisk together sauce ingredients. Place chicken in an aluminum-foil pan. Spread the mustard mixture over the chicken and turn to coat thoroughly. Let stand 10 minutes before grilling.

Preheat grill. Place foil pan with chicken and sauce on grill and grill chicken over medium heat, turning several times, until chicken is no longer pink in the center, about 1 hour. Remove chicken from the pan and place on the grill. Sprinkle with sesame seeds and grill, turning several times, until seeds are toasted and chicken is crispy, about 10 minutes longer.

MUSTARD SAUCE

3   tablespoons Dijon mustard
3   tablespoons prepared mustard
1   tablespoon prepared horseradish
2   tablespoons red wine vinegar
1   teaspoon Worcestershire sauce
2   tablespoons honey

1   chicken (3 to 3½ pounds), cut into serving pieces, excess skin and fat removed
    Sesame seeds for sprinkling on top

GRILLED CHICKEN TERIYAKI
Serves 4

Teriyaki is a Japanese dish of food marinated in a soy sauce mixture. This recipe will appeal to those who prefer an alternative to the traditional red barbecue sauce for chicken. Marinate several hours to allow the chicken to absorb the flavors. Serve with rice.

In a large bowl, whisk together soy sauce, sherry, oil, water, garlic, sugar, and ginger. Add chicken and turn to coat. Marinate in the refrigerator, for 3 to 4 hours or up to overnight, turning several times. Bring to room temperature before grilling.

Preheat grill. Remove chicken from marinade. In a small saucepan, boil marinade for 1 minute. Grill chicken over medium heat, turning often and basting with marinade, until chicken is no longer pink in the center, about 1 hour. Serve with rice, sprinkled with green onions.

- ¾ cup soy sauce
- ¼ cup sherry or dry white wine
- 1 tablespoon vegetable oil
- 1 tablespoon water
- 2 garlic cloves, minced
- 1 teaspoon sugar
- 1 teaspoon peeled, grated fresh ginger, or ½ teaspoon ground ginger
- 1 chicken (3½ to 4 pounds), cut into serving pieces, excess skin and fat removed
- 1 cup long-grain white rice, cooked according to package directions (3 cups cooked)
- 6 green onions, including some tender green tops, sliced

GRILLED BASTED SALMON STEAKS

Serves 4

Salmon lends itself well to grilling because of its firm texture and high fat content, which keep it moist and flavorful. Serve with Cheesy Potatoes (page 218) for an outstanding company supper.

Preheat grill. In a small bowl or cup, whisk together baste ingredients. Brush salmon with baste on both sides. Grill over medium heat, turning once, until salmon flakes when tested with a fork, 5 to 6 minutes on each side. Serve with lemon wedges.

WINE-BUTTER BASTE

2 tablespoons butter, melted
1 tablespoon firmly packed brown sugar
2 tablespoons soy sauce
2 tablespoons fresh lemon juice
2 tablespoons dry white wine

4 salmon steaks (6 to 8 ounces each)
   Lemon wedges for garnish

GRILLED SALMON STEAKS WITH DILL SAUCE

Serves 4

Chinook salmon is the prized fish of the Northwest and is well loved in many parts of the country. Here salmon steaks are grilled until moist and tender, then served with a traditional dill sauce.

Preheat grill. In a large glass baking dish, whisk together lemon juice, wine, melted butter, salt, and pepper. Add salmon and turn to coat. Let stand for 15 minutes at room temperature. Remove steaks from marinade and discard marinade. Grill over medium heat, turning once, until the salmon flakes when tested with a fork, 5 to 6 minutes on each side. Pass the Dill Sauce in a bowl.

Juice of 1 lemon

2	tablespoons dry white wine
2	tablespoons butter, melted
¼	teaspoon salt
	Freshly ground pepper to taste
4	salmon steaks (6 to 8 ounces each)
	Dill Sauce (recipe follows)

DILL SAUCE

In a small bowl, stir together all ingredients. Cover and refrigerate until serving, or up to 3 days. Serve at room temperature.

Makes ½ cup

¼	cup mayonnaise
¼	cup plain nonfat yogurt
1	teaspoon snipped fresh chives
1	tablespoon chopped fresh dill or 1 teaspoon dried dill
1	tablespoon white wine vinegar
½	teaspoon salt
¼	teaspoon freshly ground pepper

GRILLED SALMON FILLETS WITH FRESH HERB COATING

Serves 4

Lively and impressive, with the flavor of fresh herbs and lemon juice, this salmon can be served for a company supper. Serve with Grilled Veggie Bobs (page 299) and finish with a Mixed Berry Cobbler (page 311).

In a small bowl, combine herbs, green onions, garlic, lemon juice, olive oil, salt, and pepper.

Preheat grill. Coat tops of fillets with herb mixture and let stand at room temperature for 10 minutes. Grill salmon, skin side down, over medium heat, until it begins to flake when tested with a fork, 15 to 20 minutes. Transfer to a platter and remove skin. Cut into serving pieces and garnish with lemon wedges.

¼ cup chopped fresh basil or 1 teaspoon dried basil

¼ cup chopped fresh parsley or cilantro

1 tablespoon chopped fresh dill or ½ teaspoon dried dill weed

4 green onions, including some tender green tops, finely chopped

1 garlic clove, minced

2 tablespoons fresh lemon juice

1 tablespoon olive oil

¼ teaspoon salt

Freshly ground pepper to taste

1½ pounds salmon fillets, with skin

Lemon wedges for garnish

GRILLED HALIBUT STEAKS WRAPPED IN BACON

Serves 4

Summer patio suppers should be easy on the cook. In this simple recipe, the bacon adds a light, salty flavor to the delicate halibut as it grills. Serve with Greek-Style Grilled Zucchini (page 297) and grilled French bread slices.

In a large glass baking dish, whisk together lime juice, olive oil, salt, and white pepper. Add halibut and turn to coat. Let stand for 10 minutes at room temperature.

Preheat grill. Remove halibut from marinade and discard marinade. Wrap 2 slices of bacon around each steak, securing with toothpicks. Grill over medium heat, turning once, until the fish begins to flake when tested with a fork, 5 to 6 minutes on each side. Remove toothpicks before serving.

Juice of 2 limes

2 tablespoons olive oil

½ teaspoon salt

⅛ teaspoon white pepper

4 halibut steaks, ¾ to 1 inch thick (6 to 8 ounces each)

8 slices bacon, partially cooked (see Note, page 80)

Grilled French bread slices for serving (see Note)

NOTE: To grill French bread, cut a loaf or baguette into ½-inch slices, brush with garlic-flavored oil, and grill until toasted, 1 to 2 minutes on each side.

GRILLED SHRIMP, SCALLOP, AND FRUIT KABOBS WITH PINEAPPLE-WINE MARINADE

Serves 4

Grilling fruit brings out the natural sweetness and intensifies the flavor. These colorful kabobs make for an appealing, eye-catching main course.

In a medium bowl, whisk together reserved pineapple juice, sherry, and vinegar. Reserve ¼ cup of marinade for basting. Add shrimp and scallops to bowl and let stand at room temperature for 15 minutes.

Preheat grill. Remove shrimp and scallops from marinade and discard marinade. Thread shrimp and scallops alternately with pineapple and melon on skewers.

Grill kabobs over medium heat, brushing with reserved marinade and turning several times, until shrimp turns pink and scallops are opaque, 5 to 7 minutes.

¼ cup dry sherry or sweet white wine

2 teaspoons balsamic vinegar

8 ounces large shrimp, shelled and deveined

8 ounces sea scallops, muscle removed (see Note, page 166)

1 can (8 ounces) pineapple chunks, drained, and ¼ cup juice reserved

2 cups cantaloupe chunks (1½-inch pieces)

KABOBS FROM THE SEA
Serves 4

These delicate kabobs of marinated shrimp, scallops, and vegetables are served on a bed of rice for a colorful presentation. Pass the Dill Sauce and consider a Layered Ice Cream Mocha Pie (page 318) for dessert.

In a medium bowl, whisk together marinade ingredients. Add vegetables and stir to coat. With a slotted spoon transfer vegetables to a plate. Remove ½ cup marinade for basting and set aside. Add shrimp and scallops to bowl and toss gently to coat. Let stand at room temperature 15 minutes.

Preheat grill. Remove seafood from marinade and discard marinade. Thread seafood on skewers, alternating with vegetables, keeping shrimp and scallops flat on skewers. Grill over medium heat, basting with reserved marinade and turning several times, until shrimp turns pink, scallops are opaque, and vegetables are tender, about 5 to 7 minutes. Serve immediately, with Dill Sauce.

MARINADE

Juice of 2 lemons
½   cup vegetable oil
½   teaspoon salt
½   teaspoon dried dill
1   garlic clove, split
2   tablespoons chopped fresh parsley

12   mushrooms, stems removed
1   red bell pepper, seeded and cut into 1½-inch pieces
½   yellow onion, cut into wedges and separated into pieces
1   zucchini, unpeeled, cut into ½-inch slices
12   large shrimp, peeled and deveined
12   large sea scallops, muscle removed (see Note, page 166)
   Dill Sauce (page 287)

GRILLED SHRIMP

Serves 4

Quick grilling of these succulent shrimp captures the real fresh flavor of the sea. Fettuccini with Basil Pesto (page 190) and Frozen Lemon Ice Cream Pie (page 317) go well with these shrimp.

In a medium bowl, whisk together olive oil, wine, garlic, salt, pepper, Tabasco, and parsley. Add shrimp and let stand at room temperature for 15 minutes.

Preheat grill. Remove shrimp from marinade and discard marinade. Thread shrimp on skewers. Grill over medium heat, turning once, until shrimp turns pink, 4 to 6 minutes. Serve immediately, with Spicy Red Sauce.

2   tablespoons olive oil
2   tablespoons dry white wine
4   garlic cloves, minced
¼   teaspoon salt
    Freshly ground pepper to taste
2   or 3 drops Tabasco sauce
1   tablespoon chopped fresh parsley
1½ pounds large shrimp, peeled and deveined
    Spicy Red Sauce (recipe follows)

SPICY RED SAUCE

This sauce is also good in a crab cocktail.

In a small bowl, whisk together all ingredients. Cover and refrigerate several hours to allow flavors to blend.

Makes about ½ cup

¼   cup ketchup
2   tablespoons chili sauce
2   teaspoons prepared horseradish
1   teaspoon fresh lemon juice
2   or 3 drops Tabasco sauce
1   teaspoon Worcestershire sauce

GRILLED PORTOBELLO MUSHROOM BURGERS

Serves 4

Portobello mushrooms have a rich, meaty flavor and chewy texture, and are a popular alternative to the usual hamburger patty. Dressed with condiments, even stalwart meat lovers can hardly tell the difference. Serve with Potato Salad Everyone Loves (page 59).

Preheat grill. Brush both sides of mushrooms with olive oil. Season generously with salt and pepper. Grill over medium heat until tender, about 5 minutes on each side. Add cheese slices for the last few minutes of cooking time.

Warm buns on grill until lightly toasted. Serve burgers in buns with tomato slices, onion slices, and lettuce leaf on each. Pass condiments.

4 portobello mushrooms, stems removed, and some of the gills scraped off the underside of the caps

¼ cup olive oil

Salt and freshly ground pepper to taste

4 ounces Havarti cheese or other cheese, sliced

4 large sesame-seed hamburger buns, split

1 tomato, sliced

1 sweet white onion, sliced

4 large lettuce leaves

Condiments of your choice, such as ketchup, mustard, mayonnaise, chopped onion, and chopped fresh basil, for serving

GRILLED TURKEY BURGERS WITH CRANBERRY SPREAD

Serves 4

Turkey burgers are healthful and satisfying, and a lean alternative to hamburger patties. Use the best-quality ground turkey for these burgers for best results. The Cranberry Spread gives a traditional flavor to the turkey.

In a large bowl, combine turkey, onion, mustard, Worcestershire sauce, poultry seasoning, salt, and pepper. Cover and refrigerate for 30 minutes.

Preheat grill. Form turkey into 4 patties and brush both sides with oil. Grill over medium heat, turning once, until pink is no longer showing in the center, 5 to 6 minutes on each side. Warm buns on grill until lightly toasted. Spread cut sides of buns with Cranberry Spread. Add patty, lettuce, and pickles and serve immediately.

1¼ pounds ground turkey
¼ cup finely chopped yellow onion
1 teaspoon Dijon mustard
1 teaspoon Worcestershire sauce
½ teaspoon poultry seasoning
¼ teaspoon salt
Freshly ground pepper to taste
Vegetable oil for brushing on patties
4 hamburger buns, split
Cranberry Spread (recipe follows)
Large lettuce leaves and sliced sweet pickles for topping

CRANBERRY SPREAD

In a small bowl, mix together all ingredients until well blended.

Makes about ½ cup

4 ounces cream cheese, at room temperature
2 tablespoons whole berry cranberry sauce
1 teaspoon orange zest

FOIL-WRAPPED CORN ON THE COB WITH LIME-CHILE BUTTER

Serves 6

Corn is juicy and tender when grilled by this method. Try the citrus-chile butter for a new taste treat. Serve with Kabobs from the Sea (page 291).

Preheat grill. In a small bowl, whisk together melted butter, lime juice, chili powder, and salt. Brush mixture on corn and wrap each cob in aluminum foil, covering completely and sealing the ends together. Grill corn over medium heat, turning with tongs a quarter turn every 5 or 6 minutes, until kernels are juicy when punctured with a sharp knife, about 25 minutes.

¼ cup (½ stick) butter, melted

Juice of 1 lime

½ teaspoon ground chili powder

½ teaspoon salt

6 ears fresh sweet corn, husks and silks removed

ROSEMARY POTATOES ON A SKEWER

Serves 4

This is an easy and convenient way to prepare potatoes when grilling steaks, lamb chops, or fish.

Preheat grill. Place potatoes in a medium bowl and add olive oil, rosemary, and salt and pepper. Toss to mix well and coat. Thread potatoes on skewers, leaving a small space between each slice. Grill over medium heat, turning several times, until potatoes are tender, about 15 minutes.

4 or 5 medium unpeeled new red potatoes (about 2 pounds), scrubbed and cut into ½-inch slices

1 tablespoon olive oil

1 tablespoon snipped fresh rosemary

Salt and freshly ground pepper to taste

GREEK-STYLE GRILLED ZUCCHINI
Serves 4

Cooks are always looking for a new way to prepare zucchini, especially in the fall, when it is abundant. It is great on the grill prepared simply with olive oil, feta cheese, and dill.

Preheat grill. Brush cut sides of zucchini with olive oil. Grill over medium heat, cut side down, 8 minutes. Turn and sprinkle with dill and salt and pepper. Grill until tender, 7 to 8 minutes longer. Sprinkle with feta and grill until feta melts slightly, about 1 minute longer. Transfer to a platter and garnish with dill sprigs.

4 small zucchini, unpeeled, halved lengthwise
   Olive oil for brushing
1 tablespoon chopped fresh dill or ½ teaspoon dried dill
   Salt and freshly ground pepper to taste
¼ cup crumbled feta cheese
   Fresh dill sprigs for garnish

GRILLED PESTO TOMATOES

Serves 4

Basil pesto is an uncooked sauce made from fresh basil, garlic, nuts, Parmesan cheese, and olive oil. Make your own or purchase a good-quality pesto. Here is another tasty way to prepare tomatoes when locally grown tomatoes are in season. Serve as a side dish with Grilled Marinated Beef Roast (page 264).

Preheat grill. Place tomatoes, cut sides down, on paper towels to drain for several minutes. Arrange tomato halves, cut sides up, in a lightly sprayed or oiled aluminum-foil pan. Season with salt and pepper.

In a small bowl, mix together pesto, cheese, and green onions. Spread mixture equally on tomato halves. Grill in the pan over medium heat, with the lid closed, until tomatoes are warmed and cheese is melted, about 10 minutes.

2   large tomatoes, halved and seeded (see Note, page 179)

Salt and freshly ground pepper to taste

2   tablespoons Basil Pesto, homemade (page 190) or purchased

⅓   cup grated Monterey Jack cheese

2   green onions, including some tender green tops, sliced

GRILLED VEGGIE BOBS
Serves 6 to 8

Kabobs are fun to make and fun to serve, presented on a large platter. Each guest gets his own skewer. The quantity of vegetables can be adjusted for the number of people you are serving. These veggie kabobs are great served along with Grilled Chicken Teriyaki (page 285). If using wooden skewers, soak in water for 30 minutes before grilling.

Preheat grill. Thread vegetables alternately by color and taste onto 6 to 8 skewers. Grill over medium heat, turning several times and brushing with baste, until vegetables are tender-crisp and lightly browned and grill-marked, 10 to 15 minutes.

2   small zucchini, unpeeled, cut into ½-inch slices

2   ears sweet corn, husks and silks removed, cut into 1-inch pieces

1   red bell pepper, seeded and cut into 1-inch pieces

12 mushrooms, stems removed

½   yellow onion, cut into 1-inch chunks

6   to 8 cherry tomatoes
    Baste for Veggies (recipe follows)

BASTE FOR VEGGIES

In a small bowl, whisk together all ingredients.

Makes about ½ cup

¼   cup vegetable oil

¼   cup balsamic vinegar

1   tablespoon Dijon mustard

¼   teaspoon salt

⅛   teaspoon freshly ground pepper

DESSERTS

CHAPTER 15

HOMEMADE DESSERTS FOR EASY SUPPERS

Desserts add the finishing touch and can be the highlight of a meal. A special dessert is always appreciated, especially following a light supper. Choose the right dessert to complement the meal. Because of calorie concerns, light, refreshing desserts are popular today.

In this chapter, you will find a generous selection of quick, simple desserts designed for cooks who have limited time or desire to make desserts. You can always depend on crisps and cobblers made with seasonal fruits, easy cakes and pies, refreshing ice cream desserts, and make-ahead cookies and bars.

Choose from the Apple-Berry Crisp (page 312), Spicy Fresh Peach Crisp (page 314), Mixed Berry Cobbler (page 311), Fresh Pear Upside-Down Cake (page 306), Upside-Down Chocolate Chip Cake (page 302), Beer Spice Cake with Caramel Frosting (page 305), and Butterscotch–Chocolate Chip Bars (page 325).

UPSIDE-DOWN CHOCOLATE CHIP CAKE

Serves 6 to 8

In this creative cake, the butter, coconut, and nuts form a caramelized topping, so frosting is not needed. Serve warm with vanilla ice cream.

Preheat oven to 350°F.

To make the topping, in an 8- or 9-inch cast-iron skillet, melt butter. Add brown sugar and water and stir until sugar dissolves. Sprinkle coconut and nuts evenly over mixture and set aside.

To make the cake, in a medium bowl, stir together flour, granulated sugar, cocoa powder, brown sugar, and baking powder. Add milk, butter, eggs, and vanilla and beat with electric mixer on low until blended. Increase speed to medium and beat for 1 minute longer. Stir in the chocolate chips. Pour batter over topping in skillet. Bake until a toothpick inserted in the center comes out clean, 30 to 35 minutes. Let cool on a wire rack for 5 minutes. Run a knife around the edges of the pan and invert onto a heatproof plate. Let skillet remain on top for a few seconds to allow cake to drop, then remove skillet. Serve warm.

TOPPING

3   tablespoons butter
½   cup firmly packed brown sugar
1   tablespoon water
½   cup sweetened flaked coconut
½   cup coarsely chopped nuts, such as walnuts or pecans

CAKE

1   cup all-purpose flour
⅔   cup granulated sugar
½   cup unsweetened cocoa powder
¼   cup firmly packed brown sugar
2   teaspoons baking powder
½   cup whole milk
¼   cup (½ stick) butter, at room temperature, cut into pieces
2   large eggs
1   teaspoon vanilla extract
1   cup chocolate chips

GIGI'S FUDGE CAKE

Makes 12 servings

This fudgy cake recipe has been handed down for three generations in my daughter-in-law's family, who serve it for birthdays and special occasions.

Preheat oven to 350°F. In a bowl using an electric mixer, cream sugar and butter. Add eggs and vanilla and mix well. Add melted chocolate and flour and beat until smooth. Stir in walnuts. Pour batter into a lightly sprayed or oiled 8-by-8-inch glass baking dish lined with waxed paper or parchment paper. Bake until a toothpick inserted into the center comes out clean, about 30 minutes. Let cool on a wire rack. Invert onto a serving plate, remove waxed paper, and frost.

1 cup sugar

½ cup (1 stick) butter, at room temperature, cut into pieces

2 large eggs

½ teaspoon vanilla extract

1 ounce unsweetened chocolate, coarsely chopped and melted

¾ cup all-purpose flour

½ cup chopped walnuts

Chocolate Frosting (recipe follows)

CHOCOLATE FROSTING

In a small saucepan over medium heat, melt chocolate and butter. Stir in sugar and enough milk to make a spreading consistency. Stir in vanilla and beat until smooth.

1 ounce unsweetened chocolate, coarsely chopped

2 tablespoons butter

1½ cups confectioners' sugar

2 to 2½ tablespoons whole milk

½ teaspoon vanilla extract

GRANNY'S GINGERBREAD

Makes 1 loaf

Sometimes the old recipes are the best, but are often forgotten over the years. Try this traditional gingerbread topped with Spiced Whipped Cream for a great fall dessert. Serve with Harvest Pork Roast (page 104).

Preheat oven to 325°F. In a large bowl using an electric mixer, beat together all ingredients except whipped cream on low speed for 20 seconds. Increase speed to medium and beat for 3 minutes longer, scraping down sides of the bowl occasionally. Pour batter into a buttered 8-by-10-inch glass baking dish. Bake until a toothpick inserted in the center comes out clean, 50 to 55 minutes. Let cool on a wire rack. Cut into squares to serve, with a dollop of Spiced Whipped Cream on top.

½ cup (1 stick) butter, cut into pieces
⅓ cup sugar
1 large egg
1 cup molasses
¾ cup boiling water
2¼ cups all-purpose flour
1 teaspoon baking soda
½ teaspoon salt
1 teaspoon ground cinnamon
1 teaspoon ground ginger
Spiced Whipped Cream for serving (recipe follows)

SPICED WHIPPED CREAM

In a bowl using an electric mixer, beat cream until soft peaks form. Beat in remaining ingredients.

Makes about 2 cups

1 cup whipping cream
2 tablespoons confectioners' sugar
¼ teaspoon ground cinnamon
⅛ teaspoon ground nutmeg

BEER SPICE CAKE WITH CARAMEL FROSTING

Makes 16 servings

Beer is the surprise ingredient that helps keep this spicy cake moist for days. We served this cake at a church coffee hour and it disappeared fast (they didn't know it had beer in it!). Served with ice cream, it's even better.

Preheat oven to 350°F. On a large piece of waxed paper, mix together flour, baking powder, salt, and spices. In a medium bowl, using an electric mixer, beat together butter and sugar. Add eggs, one at a time, beating well after each addition. Stir in molasses until blended. Add dry ingredients, alternating with beer, in 3 additions and mix well. Pour batter into a buttered 8-by-10-inch glass baking dish. Bake until a toothpick inserted in the center comes out clean, 30 to 35 minutes. Let cool on a rack and frost.

2½ cups all-purpose flour

2 teaspoons baking powder

¼ teaspoon salt

½ teaspoon ground cinnamon

½ teaspoon ground cloves

¼ teaspoon ground allspice

¼ teaspoon ground nutmeg

½ cup (1 stick) butter, at room temperature, cut into pieces

1 cup sugar

2 large eggs

⅓ cup molasses

¾ cup flat beer

Caramel Frosting (recipe follows)

CARAMEL FROSTING

In a medium saucepan over medium heat, melt butter. Add brown sugar and stir until the sugar is dissolved. Stir in confectioners' sugar. Add enough milk to make a spreading consistency. (The frosting will not be thick.)

½ cup (1 stick) butter

1 cup firmly packed brown sugar

2 cups confectioners' sugar

1 to 2 tablespoons whole milk

FRESH PEAR UPSIDE-DOWN CAKE

Serves 6 to 8

Upside-down cakes are traditionally baked in a cast-iron skillet, but an 8-inch glass baking dish can be used (see Note). This is a good cake to serve after soups or stews for a winter dessert when pears are in season.

Preheat oven to 350°F. In a heavy 9- or 10-inch cast-iron skillet over medium heat, melt ¼ cup (½ stick) butter with brown sugar. Stir until sugar dissolves and mixture is slightly caramelized, about 1 minute. Remove from heat. Arrange pear slices slightly overlapping, in a neat circular pattern on top of the caramel, in 2 layers if necessary.

In a medium bowl, using an electric mixer, beat remaining ½ cup butter with flour, baking powder, salt, granulated sugar, eggs, milk, and vanilla for 1 minute on low speed. Increase speed to high and beat 3 minutes longer. Pour batter over pears in the skillet.

Bake until a toothpick inserted in the center comes out clean, 40 to 45 minutes. Immediately invert onto a heatproof plate. Let skillet remain on top for a few seconds to allow cake to drop, then remove skillet. Serve cake warm, topped with whipped cream or ice cream.

¾ cup (1½ sticks) butter

¾ cup firmly packed brown sugar

2 firm but ripe winter pears such as Bosc or Anjou, peeled, cored, and sliced

1½ cups all-purpose flour

1½ teaspoons baking powder

¼ teaspoon salt

¾ cup granulated sugar

2 large eggs

½ cup whole milk

1 teaspoon vanilla extract

Whipped cream or ice cream for serving

NOTE: You can use a glass baking dish in place of the cast-iron skillet; melt the butter with the sugar in the preheating oven.

ANGEL FOOD CAKE WITH STRAWBERRY SAUCE

Serves 6 to 8

Purchased angel food cake topped with ice cream and this homemade Strawberry Sauce is a simple but special spring dessert. The sauce is a combination of fresh and frozen berries for a superb flavor; it's also good on ice cream, plain cake, pancakes, and waffles. This dessert is a fitting finish to a supper of Lamb Chops with Crumb Topping (page 116).

Cut cake into as many slices as needed. Top with a scoop of ice cream and spoon on sauce.

One purchased angel food cake
Vanilla ice cream for serving
Strawberry Sauce for serving (recipe follows)

STRAWBERRY SAUCE

In a food processor, slightly purée thawed berries and juice. Transfer to a medium saucepan. Add sugar, cornstarch, and orange juice to saucepan and bring to a boil over medium-high heat. Reduce heat to medium and stir until thickened and juices are clear, about 2 minutes. Remove from heat and stir in fresh berries and liqueur, if using. Let cool before serving.

Makes about 2 cups

1	package (16 ounces) frozen strawberries with juice, thawed
2	tablespoons sugar
1	tablespoon cornstarch
¼	cup orange juice
1	cup hulled and sliced fresh strawberries
1	tablespoon Grand Marnier liqueur (optional)

MINI CHEESECAKE WITH BLUEBERRY SAUCE

Serves 6

This small cheesecake is just right for a family meal. It is easy to make and will disappear quickly. For convenience, buy a ready-made graham cracker crust, or you can make your own. The pretty Blueberry Sauce makes it extra-special.

Preheat oven to 325°F.

To make the filling, in a medium bowl, using an electric mixer, beat cream cheese. Gradually add sugar, vanilla, and salt. Add eggs one at a time, beating after each addition and scraping down sides of the bowl with a spatula. Beat 1 minute on medium speed. Pour into cold graham cracker crust. Bake until set, about 35 minutes.

Meanwhile, make the topping: In a medium bowl, combine all ingredients.

Remove cheesecake from oven and spread on topping. Bake until topping is set, about 10 minutes longer. Let cool on a wire rack, then cover and refrigerate overnight. Serve with Blueberry Sauce.

FILLING

8 ounces cream cheese, at room temperature

½ cup sugar

½ teaspoon vanilla extract

Dash of salt

2 large eggs

1 9-inch graham cracker crust, homemade (page 315) or purchased, unbaked, chilled in the freezer for 10 minutes

TOPPING

1 cup sour cream

2 tablespoons sugar

1 teaspoon vanilla extract

Blueberry Sauce for serving (recipe on facing page)

BLUEBERRY SAUCE

This sauce, which can be made year-round with fresh or frozen blueberries, is good on ice cream, plain cake, cheesecake, or pancakes and waffles.

In a saucepan over medium-high heat, combine all ingredients and cook, stirring constantly, until slightly thickened, about 5 minutes. Let cool to room temperature before serving.

Makes about 2 cups

2   cups fresh or thawed frozen blueberries, rinsed and dried
¼   cup sugar
¼   cup water
½   teaspoon lemon zest
2   teaspoons cornstarch

RHUBARB CRUMBLE

Serves 6

The tart flavor and rosy hue of rhubarb make an appealing and tasty dessert.

Preheat oven to 350ºF. In a lightly sprayed or oiled 8-by-8-inch glass baking dish, combine rhubarb and granulated sugar and mix well. Let stand for 15 minutes.

To make the topping, in a food processor, combine the oats, flour, brown sugar, cinnamon, salt, and butter. Using on/off pulses, process until crumbly. (Alternatively, place in a bowl and, using a pastry blender, cut in butter until crumbly.) Sprinkle topping evenly over rhubarb.

Bake until bubbly and topping is lightly browned, about 45 minutes. Let cool on a wire rack. Serve warm or at room temperature, with ice cream.

2   pounds rhubarb, cut into 1-inch slices (about 6 cups)
1   cup granulated sugar

TOPPING
½   cup quick-cooking oats
½   cup all-purpose flour
¼   cup firmly packed brown sugar
¼   teaspoon ground cinnamon
⅛   teaspoon salt
6   tablespoons butter, at room temperature

Vanilla ice cream for serving

MIXED BERRY COBBLER
Serves 6

The flavors of mixed berries mingle together in this dessert. Any combination of fresh or frozen berries can be used. This cobbler goes together in minutes and is delicious topped with vanilla ice cream. This easy dessert is one my husband, Reed, likes to make for company so he can show off his dessert-making expertise. Thaw and drain frozen berries thoroughly.

Preheat oven to 350°F. In a medium bowl, stir together berries with ¼ cup sugar and water. Let stand 10 minutes. Melt butter in an 8-by-8-inch glass baking dish in the oven.

In a medium bowl, stir together ¾ cup sugar, flour, and baking powder. Stir in milk and mix well. Remove baking dish from oven and pour batter on top of butter. Do not stir. Spoon undrained berries on top. Sprinkle with remaining 1 tablespoon sugar. Bake until bubbly and top is golden, about 40 minutes. Let cool on a wire rack. Serve warm or at room temperature, with ice cream.

4   cups mixed fresh or frozen berries (boysenberries, blueberries, blackberries, or raspberries; see Note)
1   cup, plus 1 tablespoon sugar
2   tablespoons water
⅓   cup butter
1   cup all-purpose flour
1   tablespoon baking powder
1   cup whole milk
    Vanilla ice cream or frozen yogurt for serving

NOTE: If using frozen berries, thaw and drain thoroughly.

APPLE-BERRY CRISP

Serves 6 to 8

You can always rely on crisps for a successful and delicious dessert. This combination of apples, cranberries, and blueberries is fun to serve during the holidays, and is fabulous topped with ice cream. Invite the neighbors over for a treat.

To make topping, combine oats, brown sugar, and butter in a food processor and with on/off pulses, process until crumbly. (Alternatively, place in a bowl and, using a pastry blender, cut in butter until crumbly.) Fold in nuts.

Preheat oven to 350°F. In a lightly sprayed or oiled 8-by-10-inch glass baking dish, toss together apples, cranberries, blueberries, granulated sugar, and flour. Sprinkle topping over all. Bake until bubbly, about 45 minutes. Cool slightly, then serve warm, with ice cream.

TOPPING

1½ cups quick-cooking rolled oats

½ cup firmly packed brown sugar

½ cup (1 stick) butter

½ cup chopped hazelnuts or walnuts

6 apples such as Northern Spy, Rome Beauty, or Granny Smith, peeled, cored, and sliced (about 6 cups)

1 cup fresh or frozen cranberries, rinsed and dried

1 cup fresh or frozen blueberries, rinsed and dried

¼ cup granulated sugar

2 tablespoons all-purpose flour

BLUEBERRY CRISP WITH WALNUT STREUSEL TOPPING

Serves 6

Studies have shown that blueberries provide many health benefits and should be eaten often. They can be used on cereal, in salads, in sauces, in berry crisps or crumbles, and in ice cream or sherbet. Top this crisp with vanilla ice cream.

To make topping, combine oats, flour, brown sugar, and butter in a food processor and with on/off pulses, process until crumbly. (Alternatively, place in a bowl and, using a pastry blender, cut in butter until crumbly.) Fold in nuts. Set aside.

Preheat oven to 375°F. Combine blueberries, lemon juice, granulated sugar, and cornstarch in a buttered 8-by-8-inch glass baking dish and toss gently. Sprinkle topping over all and bake until bubbly, about 45 minutes. Cool slightly, then serve warm.

TOPPING

½   cup quick-cooking rolled oats

½   cup all-purpose flour

¼   cup firmly packed brown sugar

6   tablespoons butter, at room temperature

½   cup chopped walnuts (optional)

5   cups fresh or frozen blueberries, thawed, rinsed, and dried

2   tablespoons fresh lemon juice

⅓   cup granulated sugar

1   tablespoon cornstarch

SPICY FRESH PEACH CRISP

Serves 8 to 10

Fresh peaches in season make a delicious, juicy crisp for the family or company to enjoy. This recipe makes a lot, but don't expect leftovers. Serve with vanilla ice cream.

To make topping, combine oats, flour, brown sugar, and butter in a food processor and using on/off pulses, process until crumbly. (Alternatively, place in a bowl and, using a pastry blender, cut in butter until crumbly.) Set aside.

Preheat oven to 350°F. In a large bowl, mix together peaches, granulated sugar, tapioca, lemon juice and zest, cinnamon, and nutmeg and gently toss. Let stand for 10 minutes. Transfer to a buttered 9-by-13-inch glass baking dish and sprinkle topping over all. Bake until bubbly, 50 to 60 minutes. Cool slightly, then serve warm.

TOPPING

¾ cup quick-cooking rolled oats

¾ cup all-purpose flour

2 tablespoons firmly packed brown sugar

½ cup (1 stick) butter, cut into pieces

6 to 7 medium (about 3 pounds) fresh peaches, peeled (see Note), pitted, and sliced (6 to 8 cups)

1½ cups granulated sugar

¼ cup instant tapioca

1 tablespoon fresh lemon juice

1 teaspoon grated lemon zest

½ teaspoon ground cinnamon

¼ teaspoon ground nutmeg

Pinch of salt

NOTE: To peel peaches, cut an X in the blossom end. Immerse in boiling water for 30 seconds, then drain and let cool; skins will peel off easily.

SOUR CREAM PEACH PIE
Serves 6

This luscious pie with fresh peaches is a perfect finishing touch for a summer supper. Buy a prepared crust or make your own.

Preheat oven to 375°F. In a medium bowl, toss together peaches, granulated sugar, and flour. Transfer to the prepared crust. In another medium bowl, whisk egg yolks. Add sour cream, brown sugar, and salt and whisk to blend. Pour over the peaches. Bake until set, about 40 minutes. Let cool on a wire rack. Cut into wedges to serve.

3   medium fresh peaches, peeled (see Note on facing page), pitted, and sliced (about 3 cups)
¼   cup granulated sugar
2   tablespoons all-purpose flour
1   9-inch graham cracker crust, homemade (recipe follows) or purchased, unbaked
2   large egg yolks
1   cup sour cream
¼   cup firmly packed brown sugar
¼   teaspoon salt

GRAHAM CRACKER CRUST

Preheat oven to 350°F. Place graham crackers in a food processor, and process to make about 1½ cups fine crumbs. In a bowl, combine crumbs with melted butter and sugar and mix well. Transfer mixture to a 9-inch pie plate and press firmly on the bottom and up the sides with your fingers.

Makes 1 pie shell

20 squares graham crackers, broken up
⅓   cup butter, melted
3   tablespoons sugar

OREGON WALNUT PIE

Serves 6

This rich, delicious pie is often called the "pecan pie of the West." It's especially good topped with whipped cream or ice cream when it's still warm.

Preheat oven to 400°F. In a medium bowl, whisk eggs. Add corn syrup, brown sugar, melted butter, vanilla, and salt and whisk until blended. Sprinkle nuts on the bottom of pie shell. Pour egg mixture over and bake for 10 minutes. Reduce heat to 350°F and continue baking until set, about 50 minutes longer. Let cool on a wire rack. Serve warm or at room temperature with whipped cream or ice cream.

3 large eggs

1 cup light corn syrup

$\frac{1}{2}$ cup firmly packed brown sugar

$\frac{1}{4}$ cup ($\frac{1}{2}$ stick) butter, melted

1 teaspoon vanilla extract

$\frac{1}{8}$ teaspoon salt

1 cup walnut pieces

1 8-inch unbaked pie shell, purchased or homemade

Unsweetened whipped cream or ice cream for serving

FROZEN LEMON ICE CREAM PIE

Serves 6

Frozen lemonade adds tartness to a creamy ice cream filling in a crispy crust. This is a refreshing summertime dessert, when light eating is in order. It goes well with Grilled Salmon Steaks with Dill Sauce (page 287).

Preheat oven to 325°F. In a medium bowl, using a pastry blender, mix wafers, sugar, and butter until crumbly. Press firmly onto the bottom and sides of a lightly sprayed or oiled 9-inch glass pie plate. Bake until lightly browned, 10 to 12 minutes. Let cool on a wire rack, then refrigerate until cold. Place ice cream in a large bowl and, using an electric mixer, beat lemonade concentrate into ice cream until smooth. Spread onto crust and freeze until firm, about 4 hours. Cut into wedges to serve, garnished with lemon slices and mint sprigs

1½ cups crushed vanilla wafers (about 40)

1 tablespoon sugar

¼ cup (½ stick) butter

1 quart vanilla ice cream, softened

6 ounces frozen lemonade concentrate, thawed

Lemon slices and fresh mint sprigs for garnish

LAYERED ICE CREAM MOCHA PIE

Serves 6

Ice cream pies are great for easy suppers because they can be made ahead. Here, two ice creams are combined and topped with chocolate sauce. Allow about 2 hours freezing time.

Place chocolate ice cream in a medium bowl and allow to soften, stirring several times. Spread into the crust and freeze until firm, at least 2 hours. Place coffee ice cream in a medium bowl and allow to soften, stirring several times. Spread over chocolate ice cream and freeze until firm, at least for 2 hours or until ready to serve. Cut into wedges, drizzle with chocolate sauce, and sprinkle with nuts.

1   pint chocolate ice cream

1   9-inch graham cracker crust, homemade (page 315) or purchased, unbaked

1   pint coffee ice cream

½   cup Chocolate Fudge Sauce, homemade (page 321) or purchased, warmed

Chopped nuts for sprinkling on top

STRAWBERRY-PINEAPPLE DELIGHT

Serves 4

For a pretty springtime dessert, serve this layered dessert with sweetened strawberries and a pineapple-sour cream mixture in individual glass dishes or parfait glasses.

4	cups strawberries, hulled and quartered
4	tablespoons sugar
1	can (8½ ounces) crushed pineapple, drained
1	cup sour cream
¼	cup chopped pecans

In a medium bowl, mix berries with 2 tablespoons sugar and set aside. In another medium bowl, mix together pineapple, remaining 2 tablespoons sugar, sour cream, and pecans. Alternate layers of pineapple mixture and strawberries in 4 chilled parfait glasses or other glass dishes, ending with strawberries.

CLASSIC BREAD PUDDING WITH ORANGE SAUCE

Serves 6

This old-fashioned dessert has become popular again and is currently featured in many upscale restaurants. Serve with the luscious homemade Orange Sauce. This is best when freshly made; good bread choices are coarse country bread, French bread or challah.

Preheat oven to 350°F. In a large bowl, whisk together eggs, milk, melted butter, sugar, vanilla, cinnamon, and cloves. Add bread and raisins and mix well. Transfer to a buttered 1½-quart casserole. Bake, uncovered, until set, 40 to 45 minutes. Serve warm, with Orange Sauce.

2	large eggs
2	cups milk
¼	cup (½ stick) butter, melted
½	cup sugar
1	teaspoon vanilla extract
1	teaspoon ground cinnamon
⅛	teaspoon ground cloves
4	cups day-old bread, cut into 1-inch cubes
½	cup raisins or dried currants
	Orange Sauce for serving (recipe follows)

ORANGE SAUCE

In a medium saucepan over medium heat, combine cornstarch, orange juice, lemon juice, sugar, and zest. Stir constantly until thickened, about 5 minutes. Add butter and stir until butter is melted. Serve warm.

Makes about 1¼ cups

1	tablespoon cornstarch
1	cup orange juice
1	tablespoon fresh lemon juice
¼	cup sugar
1	teaspoon grated orange zest
1	tablespoon butter

DOUBLE CHOCOLATE ICE CREAM SUNDAES

Serves 4

For a fun and easy dessert, spoon rich homemade fudge sauce over ice cream and top with nuts. The sauce is also good on angel food cake.

Scoop ice cream into dessert dishes and top with sauce and nuts.

1   quart chocolate ice cream
     Chocolate Fudge Sauce, homemade
     (recipe follows) or purchased, for serving
     Chopped nuts for topping

CHOCOLATE FUDGE SAUCE

This sauce uses cocoa powder, which has less fat than baking chocolate. It will not get hard when cold, so it can be kept, covered in the refrigerator, for days. It is delicious served hot or cold.

In a small saucepan over medium heat, combine cocoa powder, cornstarch, and sugar and stir to mix. Slowly stir in hot water, then corn syrup. Bring to a boil and cook, stirring constantly, until slightly thickened, about 2 minutes. Remove from heat and stir in butter and vanilla. Serve warm.

Makes about 1 cup

$1/4$ cup unsweetened cocoa powder
1   tablespoon cornstarch
$1/2$ cup sugar
1   cup hot water
1   tablespoon light corn syrup
1   tablespoon butter
$1/2$ teaspoon vanilla extract

ICE CREAM CRUNCH

Serves 8 to 10

This easy dessert is one you will make again and again. The "crunch" can be made ahead, but allow several hours freezing time after final assembling with ice cream. Serve plain, or top with fresh whole berries or a berry or chocolate sauce.

Preheat oven to 400°F. In a food processor, combine flour, brown sugar, and butter and, using on/off pulses, process until crumbly. (Alternatively, place in a bowl and, using a pastry blender, cut in butter until crumbly.) Stir in nuts. Spread on a baking sheet and bake until golden brown, about 8 minutes. Let cool slightly (see Note). Place half of the crunch in a buttered 8-by-8-inch glass baking dish. Spoon ice cream on top and spread until smooth. Sprinkle remaining crunch on top of ice cream and pat down with a fork. Cover and freeze until firm, 2 to 3 hours. Remove from freezer and let stand a few minutes before cutting into squares to serve.

1 cup all-purpose flour

¼ cup firmly packed light brown sugar

½ cup (1 stick) butter, at room temperature, cut into pieces

½ cup chopped pecans or walnuts

½ gallon vanilla ice cream, softened

NOTE: If the crumbs are too clumpy after baking, process briefly in the food processor.

COFFEE-PECAN SUNDAES

Serves 6

Keep the ingredients for these sundaes on hand for a quick, delicious dessert for any impromptu occasion.

In a medium saucepan over high heat, bring coffee and brown sugar to a boil and stir until sugar is dissolved. Stir in vanilla. Remove from heat and stir in brandy. Let cool. Place 2 scoops (about ½ cup) of ice cream in each of 6 stemmed goblets or glass dishes. Drizzle sauce over and top with nuts.

1   cup strong brewed coffee
1   cup firmly packed brown sugar
½   teaspoon vanilla extract
1   tablespoon brandy
1½ quarts vanilla ice cream
¼   cup chopped pecans

FRESH HOMEMADE BLUEBERRY ICE CREAM

Makes 6 cups

This cool and frosty summertime treat is full of flavor and is a perfect ending for a sundown supper on the patio. Serve with Refrigerator Butterscotch-Nut Cookies (page 327).

In a medium saucepan over medium-high heat, combine berries, sugar, cinnamon, and water. Bring to a boil and cook for 5 minutes, stirring occasionally.

Working in batches, transfer berry mixture to a food processor and process until smooth. Stir in lemon juice. Transfer to a medium bowl, cover, and refrigerate until completely cold, 2 to 3 hours. Stir in cream and half-and-half.

Pour cream mixture into an ice cream maker and freeze according to manufacturer's directions. Serve in bowls, garnished with mint leaves.

3   cups fresh or frozen blueberries, rinsed and dried
1   cup sugar
    Dash of ground cinnamon
¼   cup water
2   tablespoons fresh lemon juice
1   cup whipping cream
1   cup half-and-half
    Fresh mint leaves for garnish

BUTTERSCOTCH-CHOCOLATE CHIP BARS

Makes 16 bars

Chocolate chips are added to this updated version of the old favorite, called blondies. They add a welcome sweet touch to any occasion.

Preheat oven to 350°F. In a medium saucepan over medium-low heat, melt butter. Remove from heat. Add brown sugar, vanilla, and egg and mix well. Stir in flour, baking powder, and salt. Let cool slightly. Stir in chocolate chips. Spread into a lightly buttered 8-by-8-inch glass baking dish. Bake until a toothpick inserted in the center comes out clean, about 25 minutes. Let cool slightly on a wire rack. Cut into squares while still warm.

¼	cup (½ stick) butter
1	cup firmly packed brown sugar
1	teaspoon vanilla extract
1	large egg
¾	cup all-purpose flour
1	teaspoon baking powder
¼	teaspoon salt
½	cup chocolate chips

EASY BROWNIES

Makes 16 squares

Every cook has a favorite brownie recipe, but this is an especially easy one, made in one pan but yielding the same full richness. Once all of the ingredients are measured out, you will have these popular brownies in the oven in minutes.

Preheat oven to 325°F. In a medium saucepan over low heat, melt chocolate and butter. Add sugar and stir until dissolved. Remove the pan from heat. Add eggs one at a time, beating well after each addition. Stir in flour, vanilla, and nuts and beat until blended. Pour into a lightly buttered 8-by-8-inch glass baking dish. Bake until a toothpick inserted in the center comes out almost clean, about 25 minutes. Do not overbake. Let cool completely on a wire rack, then cut into squares.

2   ounces unsweetened baking chocolate, coarsely chopped
¼   cup (½ stick) butter
1   cup granulated sugar
2   large eggs
½   cup all-purpose flour
1   teaspoon vanilla extract
½   cup chopped nuts, such as walnuts or hazelnuts

REFRIGERATOR BUTTERSCOTCH-NUT COOKIES

Makes about 3½ dozen cookies

These cookies are great for keeping on hand for unexpected guests, especially during the holidays. The dough freezes beautifully for months, ready to slice, bake, and serve warm from the oven.

In a medium bowl, using an electric mixer, cream butter and sugars. Add eggs one at a time, beating well after each addition. Beat in vanilla, vinegar, flour, and salt. Stir in nuts. Chill in refrigerator for 30 to 60 minutes for easier handling. Divide the dough onto 3 pieces of waxed paper. Form dough into three 2-by-10-inch logs and wrap tightly in the waxed paper, twisting ends to seal. Refrigerate overnight. (Wrap in foil to freeze up to 4 months; see Note.)

Preheat oven to 375°F. With a thin, sharp knife, cut dough into ¼-inch slices. Place ¾ inch apart on an ungreased parchment-lined baking sheet. Bake until golden, about 12 minutes. Let cool on a wire rack and store in a covered container.

1½ cups (3 sticks) butter
1 cup granulated sugar
1 cup firmly packed light brown sugar
2 large eggs
1 teaspoon vanilla extract
2 teaspoons white vinegar
3 cups all-purpose flour
½ teaspoon salt
2 cups chopped hazelnuts or walnuts

NOTE: If frozen, remove from freezer 2 to 3 minutes before slicing.

INDEX

THE BIG BOOK OF EASY SUPPERS

THE BIG BOOK OF EASY SUPPERS

THE BIG BOOK OF EASY SUPPERS

THE BIG BOOK OF EASY SUPPERS

ABOUT THE AUTHOR

Maryana Vollstedt is a native of Oregon and graduated from Oregon State University in Home Economics. In 1952 she and her husband, Reed, started Reed and Cross, a small nursery and garden center that grew into a retail complex that included a landscape service, a florist, a gift shop, clothing, gourmet cookware, a wine shop, and a deli. This is where Maryana started her writing career in the mid-1960s by authoring the first cookbook and manual for the Kamado barbecue. She continued to write, and self-published 15 other cookbooks on a variety of subjects.

The Vollstedts sold the store in 1979 to travel and pursue other interests. Since 1995, Maryana has written *Pacific Fresh*, *What's for Dinner?*, *The Big Book of Casseroles*, *The Big Book of Soups & Stews*, *The Big Book of Breakfast*, and *The Big Book of Potluck*, all published by Chronicle Books. These books, with practical recipes and straightforward directions, appeal to the home cook and all have been best-sellers.

Maryana also writes a bimonthly food column called "What's for Dinner?" and has edited the "Kids Cook" column for her local newspaper the *Eugene Register Guard* for eight years. She is active in her community as the volunteer coordinator for a mentor program in five middle schools. She has four grown children and seven grandchildren. Maryana lives with Reed in Eugene, Oregon, where she continues to write cookbooks.

TABLE OF EQUIVALENTS

The exact equivalents in the following tables have been rounded for convenience.

LIQUID/DRY MEASURES

U.S.	Metric
¼ teaspoon	1.25 milliliters
½ teaspoon	2.5 milliliters
1 teaspoon	5 milliliters
1 tablespoon (3 teaspoons)	15 milliliters
1 fluid ounce (2 tablespoons)	30 milliliters
¼ cup	60 milliliters
⅓ cup	80 milliliters
½ cup	120 milliliters
1 cup	240 milliliters
1 pint (2 cups)	480 milliliters
1 quart (4 cups, 32 ounces)	960 milliliters
1 gallon (4 quarts)	3.84 liters
1 ounce (by weight)	28 grams
1 pound	454 grams
2.2 pounds	1 kilogram

LENGTH

U.S.	Metric
⅛ inch	3 millimeters
¼ inch	6 millimeters
½ inch	12 millimeters
1 inch	2.5 centimeters

OVEN TEMPERATURE

Fahrenheit	Celsius	Gas
250	120	½
275	140	1
300	150	2
325	160	3
350	180	4
375	190	5
400	200	6
425	220	7
450	230	8
475	240	9
500	260	10